MARCUS of UMBRIA

MARCUS *of* UMBRIA

What an Italian Dog Taught an American Girl about Love

Justine van der Leun

RODALE

© 2010 by Justine van der Leun

Rodale books may be purchased for business or promotional use
or for special sales. For information, please write to: Special Markets Department,
Rodale Inc., 733 Third Avenue, New York, NY 10017.

Printed in the United States of America

Rodale Inc. makes every effort to use acid-free ♾, recycled paper ♻.

Book design by André Mora

Library of Congress Cataloging-in-Publication Data

Van der Leun, Justine.
  Marcus of Umbria : what an Italian dog taught an American girl about love /
Justine van der Leun.
        p.   cm.
     ISBN-13 978–1–60529–960–0   hardcover
     ISBN-10 1–60529–960–X   hardcover
  1. Van der Leun, Justine.   2. Van der Leun, Justine—Relations with men.
3. Americans—Italy—Umbria—Biography.   4. Dogs—Italy—Umbria.
5. Human-animal relationships—Italy—Case studies.   6. Man-woman
relationships—Italy—Case studies.   7. Umbria (Italy)—Biography.   8. Collelungo
(Italy)—Biography.   9. Umbria (Italy)—Social life and customs.   10. Collelungo
(Italy)—Social life and customs.   I. Title.
DG55.U63V36   2010
945'.651—dc22   2009042645

Distributed to the trade by Macmillan

2 4 6 8 10 9 7 5 3 1   hardcover

LIVE YOUR WHOLE LIFE™

We inspire and enable people to improve their lives and the world around them

For more of our products visit **rodalestore.com** or call 800-848-4735

For Patricia van der Leun, obviously

1

MISTAKES AREN'T ALWAYS REGRETS.

—*A SOFTER WORLD*, JOEY COMEAU AND EMILY HORNE

MARCUS STOOD ACROSS FROM ME with a fluffy white chicken clamped in her jaws. Her body was taut, trembling, her skinny legs ramrod straight, her chest expanded, her eyes wild. She gazed past me, overwhelmed by her own stunning success. The chicken, though in a state of shock, was alive, and it shot me an imploring look from its hapless position.

"Marcus, you drop that," I hissed. Marcus looked away and held tight to her prize. Her shiny black face, which was normally small, pretty, and prim, was feral and strewn with saliva. Her floppy ears had flipped back and inside out during the struggle, and her lips were curled into a wide, perverse grin. She slowly lowered herself to the ground in the middle of the gruesome scene and wrapped her delicate paws around the chicken's legs. The grass was blanketed with feathers; some still floated mournfully in midair. Marcus threw me a guilty, sidelong glance, bird still firmly in mouth. She had plans to savor it, I could tell.

I looked ahead. A tidy stone farmhouse sat a few yards away, and this chicken belonged to whoever lived there, as did its wide-eyed companion, who was perched on a branch fifteen feet above the ground. It stared down at me. Chickens, it turned out, could be propelled to modest flight by a surge of adrenaline.

The flying chicken and I were on the same page: We had both embarked on a peaceful evening stroll, and we now bore witness to a brutal mauling. Like most brutal maulings, it had happened so quickly.

My friend Sabrina, the only English speaker in this particular landlocked area of central Umbria, and I had been involved in a conversation while Marcus had been making her usual top-speed rounds over the muddy, dark ground, under the tall pines, racing in loops, damp black snout to the soft earth. Sabrina's mother had recently told Sabrina to stop eating panettone, lest she find herself too plump to snag a husband, and had then turned to me and exclaimed, pointing at her daughter, "This one is almost forty!"

"And once she finds a husband?" I asked.

"*Then* she can eat whatever she wants!" her mother said, pushing a drawer shut with her significant rump.

Sabrina's sole wish in life was to escape from her Umbrian village to Manchester, England, where she would contentedly work as an unmarried, panettone-eating university librarian. We were discussing how she might make this dream a reality when I realized that I had not seen my dog for some time.

"Marcus, vieni qua!" I yelled. The forest was quiet and damp, enclosed like a big old room, with the trees so wide and packed that they completely obscured the sky. I turned to Sabrina, my heart sinking. I knew, suddenly, certainly, that disaster was inevitable. "Sabri, are there any chickens around here?" I asked.

Then I was running toward a thick bush and pushing apart its long branches. Light streamed in, and I stood with my hands holding the parted greenery, my head popping through, my body still in the woods. Twenty yards ahead, I saw a bucolic scene: the ancient house with its terra-cotta roof, its jade lawn, a cloudless blue sky, and a few happy hens wandering through the grass, picking up seeds and bugs, letting out contented clucks.

A few feet behind the oblivious poultry crept Marcus, her eyes hard, her movements controlled. She crouched low like a vicious feline. Her face was stone cold, dead set. It was a scene from the African prairie: the sweet antelope chomping on grass while the leopard approaches. Could the inhabitants of the farmhouse see her from their windows? Were they readying the rifle? I burst through the bushes and began to run toward the scene of impending doom, my mouth shut for fear of alerting the chickens' owners. As I was closing in, so was Marcus, and she was the superior athlete. In one fluid movement, she pounced, grabbing the closest, unluckiest chicken in her jaws just as I came within arm's length.

"Drop it," I said forcefully. I stepped forward, Marcus stepped back. I shimmied toward her, she shimmied away. She let out a guttural noise. She seemed to be experiencing a pleasure she had never before known.

"Drop it?" I pleaded. I tiptoed in her direction. She rose and sidestepped. I threw myself to the ground and began to crawl.

She stood poised with her kill, fixing me with a maniacal, impenetrable gaze. This was not the dog I knew. The little hunting dog that I had adopted quivered when a motorcycle drove by and was disconcerted by especially large flies. Once, a sheep beat her up. A particularly confident cat often successfully chased her, hissing. I had never believed her capable of violence. Now, in the face of my pointer, I saw at close range the fierce undercurrent, the animal beneath. I was extremely impressed.

Part of me felt that if she was good enough to catch the bird, she should get to taste its blood. That was what she wanted—just a sip of chicken blood, that's all. Was this the extreme, gnarled love of a mother, hoping for her child's happiness even at the expense of an innocent life? Did I care?

I did care—I cared just enough. There was a moral imperative here: I was all that chicken had in the world, and I couldn't turn my back on it. I continued to whisper furiously at Marcus. I could have touched the bony avian foot with my outstretched hand, but I knew any sudden movements would push Marcus farther away. She was considering her options, frowning as she held the game and mulled over how relatively important I was to her.

"You let it *go*," I growled.

Finally, torn, she let go of the chicken and leaped over to me. As soon as she had accomplished this—it all happened in no more than a second—she regretted her decision and tried to hop back to her gasping casualty, but it was too late: I had her by the collar.

I dragged her—muzzle coated with feathers—through the bushes again, to find Sabrina waiting.

"Sabrina, I think she may have killed their chicken!" I said, the dog straining in my hands. "Do we go to the house and say something? What do we do?"

Sabrina was from these parts. Surely she would know the best way to proceed. She was a full-grown professional woman, well educated, composed, and polite. She paused for a moment to consider our course of action.

"We run," she said, and all three of us took off through the wilderness.

PERHAPS THE ONE UNIVERSAL HUMAN experience is surprise: Life just doesn't go the way you think it will. For example, I did not ever expect to find myself running at top speed through the depths of the Italian boonies with a bloodthirsty canine ward. The sequence of events that led me there began almost a year earlier, on a muggy July evening in Collelungo, a two-hundred-person sheep-farming village in Umbria. I was visiting the local bar, which, on its own, was not something for which I'd ever really prepared.

An Italian café at night is a man's world, loud and stinky, especially on a muggy July evening in a landlocked town, when the air is heavy with the aroma of thirty poker-playing septuagenarians who spend their days tending to livestock, smoking unfiltered Benson & Hedges Blues, and drinking espresso.

I had never before set foot in such an establishment, but there I stood, in the center of it, wearing my shipshape blue dress. I tried to maintain the outward impression of composure and nonchalance. I did this every day, I told myself. Nothing out of the ordinary here. Just a roomful of foreign farmers staring at me like I'm the lone member of a peculiar, arcane species. Just a tall American girl in a patterned blue sundress standing at the edge of a packed bar in an Umbrian village where nobody new ever passes. But it was too late to abort mission, to back out of the smoky den, to walk off down the dark, curving road. Instead, I would brave the awkward entrance; after all, I had come here for a reason.

In the corner, I spotted my mark: a tan young man wearing an unfortunate lime green, long-sleeved shirt and playing darts with a group of teenagers. He had been strutting around town in his worn-out blue jeans and black T-shirt, wearing a heavy silver chain around his neck, flashing a dimpled grin, and ignoring me like a champ. The first time I'd noticed him, I'd been gripped by a novel sense of intense desire. I only had three weeks; I needed to meet him now.

For someone determined, however, I was also painfully shy. I ordered a Campari and soda and looked straight down at the counter, rendered suddenly incapable of expression or movement. Seduction had never been my strong suit.

But you don't meet someone with your back turned. Mustering up all courage possible, I slowly—casually—walked to the colorful wall of magazines—one on motorcycles, a few on horses, several on women's high fashion, two on cooking, and a row of exceptionally raunchy pornography. When I turned back, I caught the man's eye. I counted to three. He was trouble—he was wickedly good-looking—and so I, of course, was all in.

He walked straight over and extended his hand. "I am Emanuele," he said with a thick accent. There was a hitch in my plans: In the fantasies I had entertained since I'd first seen him a few days earlier, he had spoken perfect English with a musical Italian lilt. In real life, it turned out, he wasn't actually fluent.

"Justine," I said, taking his rough and callused hand. We stood facing each other for a moment, smiling. I felt everyone in the bar zoom in on us. "May I have a cigarette?" I asked. I didn't smoke, but I could, just to get out of there.

"Certo," he said, and slowly led me to the side patio, which was mostly empty. We each leaned against a separate stack of plastic chairs, the dark valley below and the little town lit up beyond.

"So, what do you do?" I asked, holding out the cigarette for him to light.

"What I do?" he asked.

"What do you do for work?" I asked.

"Oh," he said slowly, and then stopped to reflect. "I am . . . *giardiniero*. Gardener?"

"A gardener!" I exclaimed. How do two people who don't speak the same language have a light getting-to-know-you chat? I would have to improvise. Emanuele the gardener looked at me calmly; clearly our linguistic differences didn't bother him in the least. I adjusted my dress.

I wanted to see Italy during my vacation, I said. Sadly, I had no mode of transportation. I smiled hopefully.

"You want see my cown-tree?" he asked. I nodded.

"Okay," he said. "I must get the *chiavi* for car."

Apparently Emanuele the gardener was one for seizing the moment. It was eleven p.m. My mother's irritated face popped into my mind. *Going out with a man just like that?* she scolded. *No! Say you're busy until tomorrow.* Ignoring the senselessness of playing head games with a non-English-speaking gardener whom I had just clumsily ensnared, I yelled out, "Not now!"

Emanuele pivoted back swiftly, puzzled.

"Tomorrow?" I asked, recovering.

"Okay," he shrugged. He was an agreeable one, this dark-eyed gardener. "Tomorrow night, I carry you to Todi."

I went back to the villa, overwhelmed, and sat alone in my bedroom, waiting impatiently for the day to end and the next one to begin.

I HAD GONE TO ITALY to take a break from New York City, where I had lived for the past seven years. An old acquaintance who owned a hotel had invited me to spend a month in his village, and I'd jumped at the chance.

An imposing Russian named Boris greeted me at the Rome airport. He stood six and a half feet tall, wore an American flag bandanna around his head, and had the look of someone who had killed ferocious animals and probably human men with his bare hands.

"You want *caffè*?" he asked. I shook my head, groggy from the overnight flight, and he grabbed my suitcase and ushered me out to a gleaming silver Mercedes. I leaned against the window, and Boris fired up the engine and sped down the A1 Autostrada del Sole, the highway of the sun. As Boris executed a series of tight and sudden turns, the bright *ipermercati* and stinking gypsy encampments of Rome faded into flat farmland, stretching wanly from the highway.

A silent hour later, we flew up a slope, took a quick left, and zoomed by a white sign that read in no-nonsense black letters, COLLELUNGO.

"Welcome in Collelungo," Boris said grimly. Ko-lay-*loon*-go.

On each side of the street, vast fields stretched out, green, brown, gold, each square plot carved perfectly into the landscape. A worn old man on an azure tractor was tilling his earth. We zipped by mud-covered pigs, lolling in the shade under the watch of a grizzled farmer in high rubber boots, and a group of captive grazing deer, and we turned onto a dirt-and-gravel road. Bouncing along, I felt a bit like royalty, protected from the glaring sun and billowing dust in the cool, leather-lined backseat of a luxury car.

We arrived at a secluded hilltop with two new villas and a sparkling pool. Boris led me up a small path to a two-bedroom stone structure with high, wood-beamed ceilings. He nodded stoically as he dropped my bags in the open living room and then departed. I heard the Mercedes barrel down the road, and saw it moments later climbing up the next hill, a little silver toy car in the distance.

Gazing out at the hill, I understood why they called Umbria *il cuore verde dell'Italia,* the green heart of Italy. The hills were covered in thick blankets of pine, each tree indistinguishable from the next, each branch choked with needles.

I found a bottle of red wine, poured a glass, and took it out to the terrace, a flat cement space with a bright blue tiled table and four wrought-iron chairs. Across the small valley rose a large and improbably round hill. The air was hot and dry, and all was still but for the intermittent sounds of insects chirping. I was alone in a foreign place. No Internet, no phone service. I felt a familiar, disconcerting sensation, the passing sort that you forget about until it emerges again, by surprise. After the bustle of travel, I sat down, took a breath, gazed out at the exotic landscape beyond, and wondered in a mute panic: Now what?

Now, two unexpected things: first, grown men gallivanting around a pool stark naked. Second, a cake race.

SINCE THERE WAS AN AZURE pool just below my villa, and since it was sweltering, I decided to take a dip at around noon on my second day in Collelungo. Though we were in the hills, the air was so unyielding that when a rare breeze passed, you let out a moan of relief. I carried my towel down to the water.

"You have arrived!" my host, a Neapolitan named Sergio,

exclaimed, emerging from his own poolside villa, a sarong wrapped around his substantial waist. He kissed me on both cheeks. "How did you sleep?"

"Great," I said. Actually, I had spent half the night staring at the ceiling and repositioning the weak fan.

"I'm happy to hear it," he said. "Listen, I prefer to be *nudo* when I swim. For you, is this a problem?"

"Oh goodness, of course not," I said.

"It's important," he said, undoing his sarong, "for me to feel liberated."

Soon thereafter, two Roman friends of Sergio's—a man and a woman in their forties—came up from the villa. They waved at me and stripped off all their clothes.

"Also, I would like for you to be the judge for the town cake contest," Sergio said. I had no idea what that was, but I agreed.

"Excellent," he said, diving into the pool.

⁓

THE NEXT DAY, SERGIO EXPLAINED Il Concorso della Torta, or the cake contest. I had arrived in July, *festa* season in Italy, during which each village celebrates the glory of its existence by throwing dozens of outdoor dinners and setting up fairs, performances, dance parties, motorcycle races, and the requisite somber march through the center of town while carrying representations of Gesù and Maria Madre.

The villagers plan their lives around these events. Sergio had wrangled a spot on the planning committee for the cake contest, and as such he had selected all his foreign friends as judges, surely angering the townspeople in an attempt to impress upon them that he was a great sophisticate. On my third day in town, I accompanied Sergio to the local bar, where he was meeting with two other members of the committee.

The bar, Le Stelle, sat at the edge of the village on Via Todi, the street that connected the nearby city of Todi to main roads and highways. Sergio and I sat down at a white plastic table on the patio. The other committee members, two young women with notebooks and clipboards, joined us and began discussing something with Sergio. I gazed over the railing. The slope dropped sharply beyond the bar into a deep valley and then rose up again. The valley was alternately thick with trees and cut into neat farmland, tiny vegetable plots, olive groves. Above it sat another small town, punctuated by a delicate bell tower.

While Sergio and the women talked, several men were attempting to change a lightbulb in one of the fixtures hanging high above the bar. One short, balding fellow with bright blue eyes was sucking on a cigarette and talking nonstop as a pair of twins—one fat and one thin—steadied a ladder.

"Che stupidi!" said the blue-eyed man. He thought they were doing it wrong.

A tall, skinny boy with straw-blond hair tucked beneath a trucker hat was alternately puffing on a cigarette, climbing toward the light, and staring at me hungrily. I averted my eyes.

As the lightbulb change evolved into some sort of loud Italian drama that I could not comprehend, another young man stepped out of the bar. He lit his own cigarette and paced around the ladder. Then, losing interest, he walked over to the table and sat down in the seat next to me, leaning back, legs outstretched. He didn't acknowledge my presence, or anyone's, really. They all continued talking as he smoked and listened.

I looked on nonchalantly. Blasé, controlled, taking it all in— the new language, the blooming surroundings. Inside, however, I was engulfed in flames; from my belly to my neck, I was burning.

The man next to me frowned and ignored me entirely. I snuck a look. Two silver hoop earrings à la George Michael, a chain around his neck—those are never positive signs. Danger, cautioned my brain.

Yes, please, chirped my body. He had a sweet, boyish face, bow lips, dimples, wrinkles across his forehead, a deep tan. He was in his late twenties, I guessed, and rugged, unshaven, with callused hands. His eyes were large and dark, with heavy lids, slanting imperceptibly downward to give him a sympathetic expression. He wore blue jeans, a white T-shirt, and worn brown leather sandals. Nothing special, my brain suggested. My body grabbed my brain in a choke hold and hissed, We must have him, you fool. No matter what, he must be ours. I sat nodding as the cake discussion ended, and then drove back to the castle with Sergio.

The next day, Sergio invited me to the town lunch. The entire population of Collelungo conversed and ate at picnic tables outside the central schoolhouse. Across from my allotted seat was the man from the bar, silver hoops and all, sitting in a slouch. I followed suit.

We were served antipasto by local women carrying large tinfoil trays: fried breaded vegetables, gigantic olives stuffed with meat, crostini covered in marinated mushrooms, garlicky tomato bruschetta, salami, prosciutto, capicola—the pig, every which way. I sat there, outwardly composed, picking at the vegetables.

"So, what does everyone here do?" I asked Sergio.

"They're all lazy, good for nothing," Sergio said in English, which nobody understood. "He's a cabinetmaker, but he doesn't really work," he gestured at the balding, blue-eyed man from the bar. "These guys go to a factory or something," he pointed to the two dark-haired men. "That one is in construction," he said of the sinewy blond who had stared at me from the ladder.

"And him?" I gestured subtly at the object of my obsession.

"He's a real artist," Sergio said. "A musician."

I had spent my whole life developing a healthy—some might say epic—sense of irony. And for what? Faced with an Italian musician, I was helpless.

That night, I lay in bed and imagined rolling down a hill with the musician, bodies intertwined. Since it was a fantasy, the grass was pillow soft and we were not injured during our cascade, and when we reached the bottom, we kissed passionately.

The next day, I reminded myself that I was not here to attempt to captivate Italian musicians who displayed no interest in me anyway. This was not Cancún. Therefore, I was going to concentrate my energies on reading and writing.

But none of my intellectual pursuits could save me. On the evening of the cake contest, I dressed in a blue cotton shift and walked down to the village center with my heart pounding and my palms sweaty. I knew I had a chance at seeing the musician again.

The townspeople were gathered outside the grocery store in anticipation of something. I peered into the crowd, and there, in the center, stood the musician, wearing leather sandals and holding a white plastic megaphone. He was announcing, with vigor, the details of the current activity. I stood to the side, awaiting the athletes, or cars, or horses. Or maybe it would be a motorcycle race, at top speed, down the steep hills. The people began to applaud.

I turned around: A rotund, freckle-faced thirteen-year-old boy wearing a straw hat bobbed along on the back of a meandering donkey. The boy held in his mouth the end of a silver spoon upon which balanced an egg. For the entire length of the block, the crowd went wild as the boy, deep in concentration, steered the animal toward the finish line. When he had arrived with an intact egg, another young boy set off on his own donkey. Ultimately, there was a total of two donkeys in attendance, so the boys competing had to trade off. At least you could say that these people were not focused on instant gratification.

I, on the other hand, would have loved instant gratification. I tried to will the musician to meet my gaze, which he eventually did. For a few seconds we both stood still, separated by a donkey, a crowd, and twenty feet of sidewalk. And then he was swept up by the mass of people on the street. I exhaled, delighted, and headed to my post at the cake contest.

The contest was held in the one-room schoolhouse, where two long tables had been pushed together. Local women brought their cakes, which, with the exception of some round fruit-and-nut numbers, were elaborately decorated. It was the summer of the Italian World Cup victory, and one woman had crafted a green sheet cake in the shape of a soccer field, complete with small plastic goals and a tiny ball embedded in an Italian flag made of frosting. There was a chocolate cake covered in candied red roses, a white powdered cake decorated with fresh-picked pink and purple lilies, a large tiramisu with the word *Collelungo* perfectly punched out on top, a cake displaying a to-scale rendering of the town chapel. There were thirty-seven cakes in total, and the judges' panel, made of four Americans, two Brits, a Dutchwoman, and a token local man, was prepared for a taste test. Organizers brought us forkfuls on plastic plates, which we were to eat and score.

About ten cakes in, the judges experienced a collective bout of sorrow. It seemed unlikely, but was apparently entirely possible, that every single cake produced by the inhabitants of an Italian town would be repulsive. By the time we'd reached the twentieth cake, we were desperate, and a little physically ill. These contestants, these kind people, most of whom looked to be very promising bakers, with their soft tummies and jolly faces, were cursed. Not one of them had learned to make a tasty, or even edible, cake. Instead, their wretched creations were dry and flavorless, or strangely flavored, sweet but cloying, with the faint scent of chemical pistachio. The filling either had too much or too little sugar, and nobody had managed to coat their cake in smooth, creamy frosting. Rather, the stuff crumbled and cracked. Cakes that contained nuts were mealy, and the fruit tarts tasted of cheap apricot jelly. The Collelungese milled about the room innocently, the whole deprived lot of them having never tasted a decent cake.

"I'm going to vomit," whispered an American to my left as she scored a cake without taking a bite.

"You have to taste them before you rate them," I growled. "It's not right."

Morals fade when things get tough, and by cake twenty-six, I too had begun to rate them without so much as a sniff.

In the end, the winner triumphed only because of the aesthetic accomplishment of her creation. We foreigners awarded top honors, one hundred euros, to a petite blonde who had decorated her sheet cake with a butterfly made entirely of fruit floating in a sky of kiwis. Its wings were a medley of peaches and currants, green grapes, straw-berries, and nectarines, and its body was made of blackberries. It even had eyes of round candy and a smile made of red licorice. We figured that the face alone warranted a victory.

CRAP CAKE WAS A MINOR disappointment compared to the glaring absence of the musician. I figured that he would arrive, see-ing as the whole of the village was packed into the schoolhouse. I wandered out, pushed through the crowd, and stood on the steps, searching for him on the lawn, but he was a no-show. I looked down at my blue shift. I had brought only one dress with me—I had to meet him that night, during its premiere appearance.

Sergio was heading to the bar, so I accompanied him down Via Todi. Outside Le Stelle, dozens of hatchbacks were crowded into tight spaces lining the road. I followed Sergio past the loiterers stand-ing by the door in a thick haze of cigarette and cigar smoke. And it was that night, at that bar, as I stood stiffly by the magazine rack, that the musician approached me.

THE EVENING OF OUR DATE, I put on an ivory sundress borrowed from an American acquaintance in the villa below and waited. And waited. The sky grew dark. I waited. I slumped in an armchair. I tried to read a magazine and threw it to the floor. I reapplied eyeliner. I whimpered. I waited. It began to pour. I waited. Finally, in the distance I made out a white tin box on wheels chugging up the hill, its little lights dim. I slogged through the muck to the edge of the driveway. There he was, my gardener-prince. He got out of the car. Was he shorter than I? Not quite. Was he wearing a tunic? He was. These were details. We kissed on both cheeks.

"I take you to see Todi," he said, referring to the nearest city for miles. "But first, I must stop at my boss house."

Ahi Velasquez, dove porti la mia vita, crooned a melancholy old Italian on the radio. I told Emanuele that I loved the song. It was written from the point of view of a lowly sailor, one far from home and under the command of a great Spanish explorer, making his way across the ocean to conquer new worlds, Emanuele explained in labored, broken English. "Oh Velasquez, where are you carrying my life?" The white car clamored along, past thick woods and broad fields lit by lightning.

The boss's old stone house was a gloomy-looking rectangular structure off a main road somewhere on the way to Todi. In the thunderstorm, the place was especially foreboding, the swaths of land beyond it black. I could hear the problem: The lightning had shorted the alarm system, which was letting out high-pitched electronic whoops. A man appeared at the front door, holding a flashlight.

"Hello!" he called cheerily in a British accent. "Sound won't stop!"

As we made our way to the house, through the flooded dirt driveway, I looked to my left. An enormous creature was barreling through the dark. I squinted as it made its way closer, and just when I realized that it was a dog, it pounced.

"Is Bianca," Emanuele hollered down as he went into the house. "She is crazy."

The immense white dog threw her paws over my shoulders, and we stood like ballroom dancers in the moonlight. Then she slid down my body, performed the universal canine boogie of delight, and ran away. I looked at the white dress. It was streaked with lines of mud. The alarm screeched on.

I sat in the car until the sound stopped, impotently dabbing at the dress. Emanuele soon returned bathed in sweat and dirt, wearing just a white undershirt, his button-down in his arms. He shrugged; the incident seemed unremarkable to him.

"You want to go to the pub now?" he asked.

I gestured to my muddy dress.

Instead, we drove up to Todi, perched at the top of the highest hill for miles. Emanuele parked the car, and we navigated on foot through tight cobblestone alleyways until we emerged at the base of a dark chapel. We could see the lights of all the villages rolling up and down into the horizon. We sat at the top of steep stone steps that led to a path some two hundred feet below, and Emanuele showed me photos on his cell phone of his nephew and his horse. Emanuele was pleasant enough, I thought. He would do for a casual romp.

On the way back to the villa, Emanuele stopped the car in the middle of the empty dirt road and turned to me. He cupped my face in his hands and kissed me.

Two days later, when the English boss had returned to London, we made our way to the now-vacant estate. There, we stripped and climbed in the hot tub, which sat slightly elevated on a vast expanse of flatland punctuated by small tracts of dense forest.

"I now know what they mean when they say 'Italian Stallion,'" I said.

"What is Italian Stallion?" Emanuele asked. We had some issues with cross-cultural humor.

"Stallone italiano?" I guessed.

Emanuele grinned widely. "I like this! I am . . . Italian Stallion."

Over the next three weeks, my days were spent either with Emanuele or awaiting him. Every evening, we landed at the only restaurant in the vicinity, a modest pizza-and-pasta joint called Rosa dei Venti that looked out over golden hills. I always ordered the crispy, cheesy, verdant arugula pizza, sprinkled with *parmigiano,* while Emanuele went for the sausage pie. Emanuele promised to repair the broken fence around an innkeeper's property in exchange for a private room in the nearby town of Morruzze, where we could stay without all of Collelungo spying through the shutters.

"They are expert of gossip," Emanuele noted of the ladies who sat on the outskirts of the piazza, craning their arthritic necks as we drove through town.

The room in which we conducted our loud affair was a simple, rigorously clean space with a bed and a shared bathroom out in the hall. It was owned by a pair of identical twins who replaced the towels every day. Nobody ever stopped by. The window looked directly at an ancient red chapel, over roofs shingled with terra-cotta, and into the Umbrian expanse. Looking down, I saw a balcony covered in herb plants and a slim, cobblestone alleyway.

"Sei bella da morire," Emanuele said as we lay together. "Sei bellissima."

I was so beautiful he could die! I faked modesty. "No, I'm not," I said feebly.

Emanuele became cross; subtlety usually gets lost in translation.

"I tell you you are beautiful because is true," he said. "I don't tell you for you. I tell you because I think it. If you have no good breast, I don't say, 'Oh, you have good breast.' Because it's not true."

"I'm sorry, my love," I begged. "And thank you."

Emanuele carried with him an acoustic guitar, which leaned against the *pensione* wall. He picked it up and lay back on the bed, brown and shirtless. There, with the hills beyond him, he began to strum and sing, his voice at once soft and gravelly. His silver hoops, his dimples: I sat at the edge of the bed on my knees, gazing at him. He was working on a song for me, in which he discussed our mutual destiny—mysterious, confused. We aren't born twice, he sang in Italian. We only own the present moment. And if he had the courage of an ancient warrior (*un guerriero antico*), he would make of me not a glorious conquest (*una conquista gloriosa*) but the most beautiful pearl in all the world (*la perla più bella*).

I thought about my little, furiously hot apartment in New York, and about the boys at the coffee shop with their subscriptions to *Harper's* and their iPods playing Neutral Milk Hotel. I wondered if we were indeed bound together, Emanuele and I. I wondered if he was my bedimpled, melodic destiny. He shot me a lazy smile. I figured I could give this thing a try.

If there is in fact such a thing as a cosmically mandated path, I was skipping dumbly down it in my underwear, to an Italian folk soundtrack.

MY LAND IS BARE OF CHATTERING FOLK;
THE CLOUDS ARE LOW ALONG THE RIDGES,
AND SWEET'S THE AIR WITH CURLY SMOKE
FROM ALL MY BURNING BRIDGES.

—DOROTHY PARKER

THREE YEARS EARLIER, I HAD arrived for my first day on the job at a lifestyle magazine in midtown Manhattan. According to television shows, magazine offices were glossy and modern, with white walls and pops of bright color, models gliding around clutching portfolios, slick editors swaggering across the spotless art deco tiles. But when the elevator opened on the twenty-eighth floor, I stepped onto worn gray carpet and was enveloped in air thick with estrogen and chemical geranium. Several rickety green chairs sat unused in the foyer, and two doors led into the offices. At the main desk sat an elderly woman with a curled black bob and thick glasses.

"How may I help you?" she asked.

"I'm Justine van der Leun," I said. "Starting work today."

"Josephine?" she strained.

"Justine."

She dialed a number. "Oh, okay, I have a Josephine here, okay?"

This was our receptionist. I would soon learn her habits: burning popcorn in the microwave, cloaking the windowless bathroom with floral room fresheners, answering the phone only 40 percent of the time. She would never learn my name.

"This is Justine," I said, picking up my ringing phone, a year into my time at the magazine.

"Justine . . . you . . . hello? Is this Jennifer?" she asked.

I had gone into publishing because I wanted to be near words, and because I possessed a dreadful knowledge of magazines. Since the age of twelve, I'd pored over *Sassy, Seventeen, Glamour, Mademoiselle, Marie Claire, Elle, Vogue, Jane, Star, In Touch, InStyle, Lucky, Domino, Harper's Bazaar, Allure, Vanity Fair.* I also remembered every useful tip I'd ever scanned: I knew that you were supposed to brush your teeth for exactly two minutes (and brush your tongue, too), that you should flush the toilet in a public restroom with your foot, that conditioner goes on the tips of the hair, and that you should bask in the steamy shower before shaving. I knew that a dull razor was more dangerous than a sharp razor, that you should exfoliate dry lips with a washcloth before applying lip balm, that Botox could be injected into the tip of the nose to raise it up, that men appreciated a woman who ordered a steak in a restaurant, that rolling up clothing gave you extra room in your suitcase, that some women styled their pubic hair in the shape of a heart, that empowered women made their own money, that empowered women were fine with having a man take care of them, and that vixen red lipstick would always come back into style but that one should tread lightly when trends dictated the loveliness of plaid. I knew that men paid by women's magazines to be anonymous male correspondents were always overly emotional and in no way indicative of real men, that women who survived sexual assaults in third-world countries often got to form bracelet-making cooperatives sponsored by first-world philanthropists, and that activists were to be photographed standing tall and unsmiling, preferably with a group of their supporters behind them. I learned that I was to love my beautiful, feminine body, and if I was a woman of color, I was to embrace my ethnic look. I was not expected, contrary to glaring implication, to look like the waifish, silky-haired nymphs lolling around in designer clothes in fashion shoots and advertisements. I knew the secrets of Parisian perfumers and that men were aroused by the scent of bacon. I knew that if you craved a jumbo frosted muffin, you could supposedly satisfy the craving by eating a handful of walnuts. If you craved a triple fudge sundae, you might try a cup of yogurt with some fresh blueberries. Whenever you wanted a slice of pizza, you were to instead be happy with seven baby carrots dipped into a tablespoon of hummus. This was how you could lose weight easily—not that you had to, since you should be comfortable with your curves.

I knew all this, and so very much more, not just because I had read it once over the years, but because I'd read it hundreds of times, because magazines lulled me to sleep. They provided a reliable respite from the world. Sometimes, after reading a newspaper article about young tin miners in the Congolese jungle, I found myself reaching, unconsciously, for a gossip magazine. They were like chasers—making the bitterness of life go down easy—and they were where I'd be working.

Everyone took their job seriously. The junior employees toiled in a central maze of cubicles while the bigwigs had windowed offices along the floor's periphery. The ceilings were low and dotted with fluorescent lights, and the walls were hung with blowups of cheerful magazine covers.

Most people were invested in the ethos of the magazine; they were believers. They typed up memos and stayed up late at night pitching new ideas. They wanted to help build the self-esteem of two million readers. They wanted to succeed, and to move on to become health editors and beauty directors and writers at large and editors in chief. When I walked through that door and sat down at my new desk, I also nursed these ambitions.

But my ambitions soon faded. Because if you wanted to do any of those things, you had to work with others. And others, it turned out, were utterly impossible.

At one point, the boss asked me if I'd be interested in a job in the fashion department. The fashion department was a materialist's dream, because corporations owned by our lead advertisers curried favor with fashion editors by sending them on trips to Paris and showering them with expensive dresses and flat-screen TVs. I nursed a mania for expensive clothing, and I crept over to the cubicle where the departing junior editor sat and asked her what, exactly, her job entailed.

Later in the day, I was beckoned to the fashion director's office, a wide carpeted room jammed with gifts. It was warm and smelled of lilac. The director, her hair blown into a casual wave, wore what I would learn was one of an assortment of wrap dresses. She reminded me of a large feline that vacillated between two states: contentment and violence. She wore lovely musky perfume.

"You missed a major step today when you considered taking a job as my assistant," she said, straightening. "*Me*."

Who did I think I was? How high did I think I could climb without her support? I had always hoped to avoid crying in a ladies' room while wearing an adorable outfit, but it was probably a universal and unavoidable experience, so I proceeded to do so, muffling my sobs in my shirt.

Two weeks later, I overheard the fashion director say, "The world is about being truly *kind* to one another."

Meanwhile, I was seated in a vortex of lunacy. One assistant who shared a cubicle wall with me wept often, her voice hushed as she hissed to her sister over the phone. "She's my mother. My *mother!*"

It didn't help my mental state that I was in charge of the Letters page. The main challenge of this gig was finding coherent and relevant e-mails among the thousands we received each month. It's well known in the world of magazines that the vast majority of people who write to publications are clinically off their rockers, though as far as I know, nobody has theorized as to why, exactly.

There was, for example, Donny: *Let me keep it short and simple, I see thinks which i have never seen it any where else. I see comparitevely big dreams which cannot be regaraged as scary nightmares. i can mail whatever i have seen. Plz, help me, for christ sake.*

Then there was Neda: *I am a writer first and foremost. With that out of the way, Hi.*

Every day, the in-box was filled with notes from people from around the globe, begging for help, for relief, for someone to listen to their tragic tales. People were stuck in bad marriages in Pakistan, gay and closeted in Algeria, looking for their dead husband and brother in Tennessee. Some were mad, some were illiterate, and the only person I could ever help was a woman in Ghana who desired for teeth whitener. Sometimes, a mentally ill woman named Barb called me on the telephone and ranted about the world until I hung up.

When I wasn't avoiding Barb or writing a trend piece, I was taking the minutes of our weekly meetings. At one meeting, the boss sat at the head of the table, flipping through the week's pitches. Traditionally, these meetings, which technically centered on the upcoming issue's theme, devolved into a series of overly personal conversations. Usually, all of us would get caught up in the moment and accidentally reveal too much. On the subject of weight, staffers who struggled with dieting argued with staffers who were naturally thin and passive-aggressively superior about it.

"I don't understand an entire diet issue," an anxious, skinny senior editor moaned. She had recently told me not to order her broccoli in her salad any longer, as the "roughage" was too much for her system to handle. "Just eat a square of dark chocolate, drink a lot of water, and have some wine when you want. Be done with it."

"It's not that easy," seethed a group of heavier ladies, each of whom had spent the past decade or three on a roller-coaster ride of weight-loss plans, scales, gyms, and trainers.

"I don't know," our muscular boss said skeptically. Her face twisted in disgust. "I have a fat, fat cousin, and he has a fat, fat wife. They really do eat. All. Day. Long." She turned to our resident anorexic, a petite jogger with a mess of red hair and a six-cup-a-day black-coffee-and-Equal habit.

"Look at her," the boss said, motioning to our anorexic. "She works on it! She may have the metabolism of a hummingbird, but when we went out to lunch, she ordered an appetizer salad, dressing on the side. You have to *work*."

There were constant battles, as well, between those who had chosen to have children and those who had chosen not to—all ostensibly for the sake of our publication, but more accurately as a way to work out personal differences under the cloak of business discussions. Our boss was happily childless ("When I see children, I just want to put them in cement," she once admitted), and she was unimpressed with the fact that mothers needed to return to their families earlier rather than later each evening. Her right-hand woman also had no children. They didn't like to do extra work to make up for the women who went on maternity leave, and they didn't appreciate having sacrificed portions of their personal lives to the office when others hadn't.

"Well, what does the woman who chooses not to have kids do?" asked the boss. "She should take a maternity leave to fulfill *herself.*"

A new mother grunted from her position at the table, her breasts sore from pumping milk into bottles, her eyes swollen from nights awake. "Right," she said, "it's a fucking vacation."

⌒⌿⌒

RULE NUMBER ONE OF KEEPING the peace: Be quiet. Do you have something that you really want to say? Because you're right and someone else is wrong, and they, and everyone surrounding them, should know just how wrong they are? Do you have an explosive, offensive opinion that you really believe in, and do you feel the pressing need to express that opinion? Do you nurse a righteous sense of how things should be, and feel obliged to let everyone know?

I did! This made it difficult for me to keep my mouth shut at advantageous moments. I lacked whatever gene or quality is necessary to comprehend that sometimes, it's easiest on everyone if you just accept the minor perceived injustices and errors occurring all about. While I appeared at first to be socially adept and gracious, I actually operated within a dysfunctional personal system in which, counter to all reason and sensitivity, I never let anything go, and never sugarcoated my opinions.

A smiling acquaintance at a cocktail party mentioned a popular book. "I just loved that book," she said. "Beautiful writing!"

"Actually, I think it's extremely overrated," I said.

Later, I wondered why she seemed to dislike me. If I was telling the truth, why would anyone get upset?

In this vein, I called another assistant "evil and abusive" to the wrong person, and word returned to her. As I followed her into the elevator so that we could have a proper confrontation on the street, I wished to get the words *Shut Up* tattooed on the inside of my eyelids. I was also disappointed to find that the majority of technical adults, myself included, were apparently perpetual teenagers.

"First of all, the trash-talking has to stop," my brand-new nemesis said. She lit a cigarette.

"I agree," I said.

"'Evil and abusive'?" she said. Her eyes began to tear. "*Evil* and *abusive?*"

"Maybe not evil," I said thoughtfully. "But abusive." At least I was consistent in my heedlessness.

We leaned against the gray skyscraper together, the wide streets crammed with cars working their way downtown. She gave me a cigarette.

"This is messy," I said, taking a drag.

"I like you, Justine," she said.

"You like me?"

"I do. I like you. I think you're *adorable.*"

We smoked in silence for a moment, and then she stomped on her cigarette and looked me straight in the eye.

"Office politics, Justine," she said. "Get in on it."

Back on the twenty-eighth floor, some regarded me with awe, the news of the confrontation having already reached the farthest cubicles. A jaded senior editor beckoned me into her office. She and her colleague wanted juicy tidbits.

"She said she *liked* me," I reported.

"I hope you said you liked her, too," the editor said. I looked at her blankly. "I hope you said you liked her, too. You said that, right?"

"You'll learn," the other said.

The next day, I had my annual employee evaluation. During the evaluation, the boss, a woman made entirely of straight lines and sharp angles, looked at me. She leaned forward. Her skin was smooth and taut, and she wore expensive pumps. She was responsible for my hiring, having received my faxed-in résumé and demanded that I be taken in. She had an air of gravity, gleaned from years of industry success. She was also eerily calm, due to loads of meditation.

"We all go crazy, but we must be like the Japanese: painfully polite even in small spaces," she said.

She was right. I was a child in her presence.

"My goal every day is to be a better person," she said. "To be *better.*"

We sat in the cavernous office for some time, looking at each other curiously.

"That's not really my goal," I said hesitantly.

"Then what is your goal?"

"I don't know."

"Well," she said, "even if that's not your goal, could you try to be your best work self?"

"Oh yes," I said. "Yes!"

I did not mean it.

∽

SOMETIMES, GETTING OFF THE TRAIN near my one-room apartment in Brooklyn, I'd see a cracked-up fellow walking down the street, screaming to himself, hands in the air. There tends to be a common theme to the one-sided conversation, and it is a defense against being wronged. The people who wrote me—or rather, who wrote the nameless, faceless entity behind the magazine's general e-mail address—were, at least from their viewpoints, being smashed around in lives that had spun out of control. They were not equipped to deal with everything thrown at them, the pointless cruelties and little inequities. Well, me neither, I thought. The office environment was for someone with a thicker skin, a more healthily diminished ego, and either a more respectful attitude toward fellow human beings or the ambition of a presidential candidate.

After just two years in the workforce, I had taken to dosing myself with a blissful prescription sleep aid at ten p.m., falling into a dead slumber, and crawling in early in the morning. I sat at my desk much like a paranoid schizophrenic, repeating internally all the ways in which I had been slighted and reworking the advice columns I edited. It was impossible to miss the similarities: A little twist in the brain chemicals, a shift in circumstances—I'd be one of those letter writers; a few years and some major disappointments down the line, I'd be yelling at my underling to double-check her spelling. "Mutato nomine de te fabula narratur," wrote Horace. "Change only the name, and this story is also about you."

AFTER I GRADUATED FROM COLLEGE in New York, I felt I should plan my life. It would no longer be acceptable, if it ever had been, to wake up hungover, or to get paid in all cash, or to wear a cowboy hat to work.

My first adult boyfriend was a man I'd known for a long time but had never dated. Now, he was suitable for my grown-up life. I devoted my energies to discovering, beneath his squeaky-clean surface, some depraved undercurrent, but there was none. He lived in a simple house in an Italian section of Brooklyn. He was a prep school teacher and a doctoral candidate in English literature, relentlessly punctual and polite. He was also funny, tall, handsome, and affectionate. His friends, all of whom I appropriated as my own, were like him: midwestern in spirit, if not also in actual fact; generous, good-natured, ethical folks dedicated to social justice and learning. They had come from a land of houses with great rooms, which were, it turned out, just huge rooms decorated with couches and distant chandeliers, and could be acquired by anyone with a decent amount of money.

These people were almost all Caucasian and had been raised Catholic or Christian, with a Jew thrown in for good measure. Some of their parents belonged to unions. They had been friends with each other since as far back as they could remember, and the girls had remained virgins until well past their twentieth birthdays. They were clear skinned, energetic, and optimistic. They worked as therapists, schoolteachers, and journalists. Nobody smoked or did drugs, and a few of them were in the midst of buying property. The couples had been together for a long time and would be married within five years and parents within seven. In theory, I had long despised this sort of happy circle. Of course, it turned out that was because I wanted in. They gave me fond nicknames and baked me cakes for my birthday. We took ski trips and threw dinner parties.

And yet. When we sat around the dinner table, drinking wine and eating chili from somebody's grandmother's recipe, I knew that they would be there forever and I would not. I could see that in the future the same group would congregate, but another woman would be sitting next to my man.

⌒∿〇

WE'RE EXPECTED TO KNOW WHAT we want, but ultimately, all I knew was what I didn't want. What I did not want, more than anything, was a golden retriever. The rupture between me and my boyfriend began here.

"They are so friendly," he said, again and again, as we paced the city streets. Whenever we saw one of those beautiful, bright faces, my boyfriend swooned, but I was not so taken. Golden retrievers had a zest for life and a silky coat, and they adored everyone. Golden retrievers loved swimming and navigated public transportation for the blind. They were the single most popular dog in the world. What couldn't a golden retriever do?

The golden represented to my boyfriend a key component of the ideal life, while it represented to me his active longing for a milquetoast existence. There was nothing unexpected about a golden retriever. You knew what you were getting: the amiable dog popularized by Gerald Ford that could be found lounging on every neatly painted front porch from coast to coast—flawless temperament, optimistic, with that flowing, buttery coat. My boyfriend also dreamed of a modest house in New England, one with a trim lawn and a hiking trail nearby. He wanted to work at a school for wealthy children, and he would not be steered away from these desires, no matter how hard I tried. The idea of a smiling purebred on an emerald green square of grass drew my throat taut. In my mind's eye, my hair was styled with a flip.

We were also having trouble communicating.

"What happened?" he asked, walking into the room where I was watching a documentary on prisoners.

"He was born in jail, and he'll likely die in jail," I explained, motioning to a man on-screen whose mother had given birth while she was in jail, and who had as an adult been convicted of a crime and sentenced to fifteen years.

"What!" he exclaimed. "As a baby, you don't have a right to be free?"

Later, he questioned what the man had done to land in lockup.

"Burglary," I said. "He's an addict."

"He's addicted to burgling!" he said.

We weren't getting through to each other.

We said, "I love you," every night and woke up together every morning; on weekends he brought me coffee and bagels. I was twenty-four and he was thirty-two, and we had been together for two years. We had fashioned an existence in which we did not fight very much. We had sex every other night. We respected each other, and our lives were intertwined. I could not have said one disparaging thing about his character. He was patient with me and accepting of my faults. We shared in chores and finances with no blowups; he was simultaneously frugal and generous, and he could make friends with anyone. He was in so many ways the picture of a perfect modern man, and all he wanted was to get married, have children, tend a lawn, teach literature to intelligent young students, and remain faithful to one person for the rest of his life.

We were supposed to be working toward something, some next step about which we never spoke. All around us, our coupled friends were securing their futures together, but we seemed to be stuck in a holding pattern. At a certain point I realized that he might be willing to stay with me forever, just to avoid dealing with the inevitable fallout.

"You know, we can't stay together," I said, sitting on his bed in the railroad flat by the park.

He looked at me calmly. "Yes," he said. He was working on his dissertation about ordinary moments in German postwar novels. "Can we talk about this later?"

Two weeks later, I reminded him of our conversation. "I was saying that I wanted to break up," I said.

"I know," he said sadly.

"I think now," I said.

"Okay," he said.

We sat in his room for a while. "Want to go to a movie?" I asked.

"No," he said.

I took a livery cab back to my place with two garbage bags full of clothes, and as I drove away, I felt released. The cramped streets of Brooklyn may as well have been an open freeway. A few years later I heard that he was living in Chicago, married to a Minnesota-born blonde, and that they had received a golden retriever of impressive lineage as a wedding present. When I got the news, I was sure that I had dodged a bullet but could not entirely justify this certitude.

SOON AFTER I LEFT HIM, I also left the magazine. I walked in one day to find a new decoration on the wall that we all looked upon. It was a phrase, stuck to the white background, composed of elegant, foot-high gold script. The assistant whom I had accused of being definitely abusive and possibly evil had plastered it there. It said, *JUST BREATHE.*

An Italian-born businessman in New York City was looking for someone to pen his memoir. He offered the job to me for a small sum, plus health insurance. There was no security, and the salary was hardly enough to live on. I handed in my resignation the next day.

4

VOLEVI LA BICICLETTA. ADESSO, PEDALI.

—ITALIAN PROVERB: YOU WANTED THE BICYCLE.
NOW, PEDAL.

IT WAS MID-SEPTEMBER. I HAD been gone from Italy for just
six weeks when I returned on a one-way ticket. Emanuele stood at the
airport gates, dressed in a sky blue shirt. He leaned on the divider,
looking up at me as I walked off the plane. As always, his smile was
slow, sweet, and bad. New York had been bleak and frantic throughout August, relentlessly hot and lonely. Wind didn't pass through my
apartment, and since I'd bought another plane ticket, I had hardly
enough money to buy food. But I didn't feel deprived; I pictured
Emanuele's face constantly and felt the anticipation of a prisoner
counting down the days to release. Emanuele, whom I had known for
three weeks, would be my salvation from sticky, competitive New York
City and from my isolation. When we met, we grabbed each other,
having written and called despite the limits of language. Now he was
in front of me, and I felt an overwhelming sense of relief.

Collelungo appeared slowly. The roads shrank, becoming cur-
vier and more narrow, and then opened up for a long streak. Then

we were surrounded again by lush trees, so dense that they blocked the light, and the road was dark. We moved into tracts of plowed ground and pig farms, onto the main street and past the bar. And finally we were in the *centro storico,* parking on a small lot in the middle of the high, ancient, interwoven stone apartments.

"O, Emanuele, ciao, eh?" an old lady shouted hoarsely. Sun and cigarettes had etched her round face with lines, and she wore thick glasses and a polyester housedress. She leaned out the window, nearly pushing over her geranium pots. Behind her, a single fluorescent light strip illuminated a birdcage with two canaries and the bald pate of a man inches from the screen of a blaring TV.

Emanuele waved. "Is my grandmother Ferrina," he said. "Our new neighbor."

"È l'americana, Joo-steen," he said to his grandmother.

"Benvenuto, Giustina!" hollered Ferrina. She peered at me, a wide, pained smile pasted across her face.

Casa nostra was a modest apartment that shared a wall with Ferrina's house. We entered by walking down a narrow cobblestone path and up five stairs. It was owned by a woman with a thick black mustache who spent her winters in Rome. Once I asked Emanuele if I might speak with her about something, and he shook his head.

"She won't understand you," he said.

"Because of my accent?"

"No," he said. "Because she is from a very old school." She would not be able to comprehend me, as a person, in general.

The interior style of *casa nostra* could be described as "all about Gesù." I put my suitcase down. A small postcard of Gesù stuck above the door, a portrait of Gesù and Maria Madre next to the fireplace, a series of framed Gesù prints lining the walls. In the bedroom, an immense oil painting of Gesù on the cross hung above the bed. Gesù *bambino,* Gesù walking on water, Gesù performing miracles, Gesù's bearded face—all captured with watercolor or acrylic, or on hazy, glossy sheets of paper pulled from books. On the bedside table sat a ceramic lamp in the shape of a pink poodle, complete with a mess of flammable magenta curls. The headboard of the old bed was wrapped in thick cobalt cotton, and the bed looked upon a television perched precariously atop a dark wood dresser. The living room and kitchen sported three armoires against the walls, and a plastic table with a faux wood top and a rose-patterned oilcloth. There were more than two hundred glasses stuffed in the cabinets.

The kitchen boasted a large brick fireplace. The mahogany shutters swung open, revealing the far-off apartments of another branch of the stone town and, down at the hills, a lone estate and its olive groves surrounded by wildflowers, several neat vineyards, and an abundant stretch of forest, the leaves of the trees in early fall turning rust and caramel.

The next morning, Emanuele went to work. I looked out the window at the bell tower, whose bell rang on the hour. Did somebody dressed in a heavy woolen cloak walk up there and pull the rope all day? I made the bed. I dusted. I unpacked my bags. The tile floors of the house were cold beneath my feet. I gathered up all the tchotchkes—the poodle lamp, the strawberry salt-and-pepper set, the ceramic rooster—and every single rendering of Gesù and carried them to the small *cantina* below the house. I carried down dozens of extra dinner plates and boxes of cups and glasses. I covered the nubby blue couch with a white sheet and made a futile attempt at scrubbing the rusty refrigerator. I arranged some oranges in a bowl and swept the entire house, then pushed through the brown and white beads that hung in front of the door to repel flies, and began to sweep the stoop. As I swept, an ancient lady made her way along the path at a glacial pace, balancing on a slim cane. She was frail and swathed in black. I heard her tapping getting closer.

"Chi sei?" she asked urgently. I looked down. She stared at me from the parking lot. We were in position for a serenade, as she was far below me. "Chi sei?"

Who was I? I understood that much. Her eyes were wide. Good question, I thought.

"Ma, non ti conosco," she said. It occurred to me that this lady had probably lived in this village for her entire life and had never seen a stranger there. "Chi sei?" I don't know you. But who are you?

I couldn't come up with any response more appropriate than a shrug. We shared a moment of uncomfortable silence, smiling weirdly at one another. Then she shrugged, too, and continued on, glancing back suspiciously.

I stopped sweeping and walked inside. There, five minutes too late, I came up with the correct answer: "Sono la fidanzata americana di Emanuele."

"Sono Giustina," I said to myself in the mirror with an expectant smile. "Sono la fidanzata americana di Emanuele."

I was five feet ten, enormously tall next to the miniature old woman, who hardly skimmed five feet. To her I must have seemed to be a member of another species—some mute, Germanic animal. It was a question of context: I was not dressed in a sarong, sipping a glass of Barbaresco on a villa balcony. She would have understood me as a tourist, then. Here I was in a dusty T-shirt, cleaning the steps of a house owned by a woman she surely knew.

For my entire life, I'd been a talker. I'd used witty retorts to control situations and to protect myself. For all my faults, I could go along with any joke, connect with all sorts of people—hedge-fund manager, trucker. I could jabber on with anybody without feeling particularly self-conscious.

Words were my passion and my trade. Now, I was relegated to shaking my head or nodding, or pointing and smiling. I felt a dawning kinship with all the non-English-speaking immigrants with whom I had conversed back in America, all those people who had been forced to subvert their personalities due to the limitations of language. They were always smiling when they tried to understand, and I now knew why—it was a submissive gesture, because a lack of language strips you of your identity and makes you feel weak.

I left the house and walked down Via Todi, then turned onto a dirt road and went through the woods. The forest fell into a valley and then rose up into another village, and I turned off into a cypress grove and sat beneath a tree, scanning my new surroundings, which seemed ever more vast.

5

WHEN YOU EVENTUALLY SEE THROUGH
THE VEILS TO HOW THINGS REALLY
ARE, YOU WILL KEEP SAYING, AGAIN
AND AGAIN, "THIS IS CERTAINLY
NOT THE WAY WE THOUGHT IT WAS!"

—RUMI

AND THEN, BEFORE I HAD fully unpacked, there was la famiglia, and they wanted to meet the person who had parachuted into their son's life.

Family: a foreign concept if ever there was one. We fear what we do not know. I did not know the meaning of family; therefore, other people's families (and, more so, my own extended family) frightened me.

I had grown up the only child of a single mother in a Japanese-style stucco house in the backwoods of a farming town in Connecticut, bordering the nation's wealthiest areas. While the other mothers in town wore tennis outfits and polo shirts, mine dressed in an assortment of heavy leather sandals and long printed skirts. My mother and I were a compact unit. We spent our weekends dressed in kimonos, reading and eating elaborate meals that she prepared. We vacationed in the desert and by the ocean, during birthdays and holidays, always just the two of us. Whatever hardships we faced, we faced them together, and alone—alone because there was no extended family to which we could turn.

My mother's family seemed to me a bitter assortment of old people in second marriages. On the outskirts, there were people vaguely related to me who seemed always to be bitching about the weather or their wayward children. Closer, there was my grandfather Gerry and his second wife, Gerri, a frail, chain-smoking pair. They lived alternately in a Palm Beach pied-à-terre and in a capacious apartment off Park Avenue, the entire space covered in white wall-to-wall carpeting and glass tables—a child's nightmare; I always stood very still and was not permitted to wear shoes. Gerry and Gerri were both tall, exceedingly thin, and handsome; they smelled of talcum powder and age, and kissed me lightly on the cheek. We saw them twice a year until Gerry passed away, at which point Gerri stopped speaking to us. She had biological children to whom she preferred to tend; she had never really liked my mother, with her unruly dark hair and her attitude.

Meanwhile, Mildred, my biological maternal grandmother, was eating chopped salads, drinking gallons of Chardonnay, and driving a silver Mercedes around Beverly Hills. Mildred had a permanent tan, a curled honey bob, and a closet full of designer clothes. Life, in her opinion, was reserved for the young and the rich. Now eighty-five and living in a retirement community, she scoffed at the elderly, at the prim and proper.

"If you don't go to happy hour, I don't know you," she said.

In the community dining room, surrounded by walkers and blue-hairs, she liked to lean in and loudly whisper, "I *don't* like old people."

Mildred had fallen in love with Gerry when he arrived at her father's favorite racetrack in a convertible with plaid interior. When they divorced in the '50s, she bundled my mother off to Los Angeles. There, Mildred married one of Las Vegas's founders, after a first date during which he drove her around in a limousine and presented her with a bottle of Chanel No. 5 the size of her head. For a time, Mildred and my mother lived at an opulent Vegas hotel, where photographic evidence proves that they sometimes dressed in matching velvet matador outfits and drank high tea on the sprawling lawn. Later, inevitably, Mildred and her second husband divorced.

"He had absolutely no sense of humor," she once told me. "But he had tons of money. Oh well, you compromise."

My mother's temperament ran contrary to Mildred's. My mother was an earnest painter when she was young, spending her days in a studio, composing modernist windmills of varying sizes in gray, green, and eggplant. She read poetry, dropped acid, and wore thrift-store clothes. Mildred, draped in chinchilla, blanched. They did not get along, and stopped speaking from the time I was three until I turned sixteen. When we were finally reunited, Mildred was just relieved that nobody had gotten fat during our separation.

"You are both so slim," she took to saying. "How did you get so nice and slender?"

I also had an uncle and several cousins whom I did not see. My mother's brother had been raised by Gerry and Gerri in New York, while my mother had stayed with Mildred on the West Coast. Therefore, my mother and her brother had never gotten to know each other, and when they reached adulthood, their lives diverged sharply. My mother went to art school in San Francisco, traveled to Europe, lived in dank downtown lofts, and taught drawing at a college in New York City, while her brother worked as a bond trader, slicked his hair back, and wore suits. Once a year, the siblings sent their nieces and nephews gifts. We all saw each other at funerals and weddings.

Then there was my father's side of the family. My father was once a handsome Berkeley student, tall and thin, with long brown hair. He fancied himself a poet and had an affinity for the melancholy sonnet. He also liked vintage Cadillacs, harmonicas, and making large-scale collages with neon paint and Mexican playing cards. After he and my mother met and married, they moved to Portugal, and then to France, where he worked at newspapers and magazines. Later, after I was born, in New York City, we all settled on Marlborough Street in Boston, where my father had a job as a book editor. He was young, bright, and impossible to work with; he had trouble hanging on to a job. No matter the subject, he was always convinced that he knew best and that everyone else was a moron. People didn't appreciate that sort of conviction.

When I was five, we moved to a white wooden three-bedroom rental on a cul-de-sac in a Connecticut harborside village. A few years before, my mother had started a one-woman literary agency so that she could make a bit of money while working from home and caring for me. It was a fluke—she merely liked books and had decided that if she could not paint, she might as well do something she enjoyed. She began by sending letters written on her typewriter to authors she admired. When we arrived in Connecticut, she happened upon a newspaper article by an unknown writer who, it turned out, had a collection of essays, which my mother sold, and which became a surprise bestseller. Cash and clients followed.

Meanwhile, my father ended up bouncing between a pornographic magazine, a small computer company, and unemployment—hardly a wannabe poet laureate's plum trajectory. He grew jealous of my mother's professional triumphs (*he* was supposed to be the literary genius; she, the struggling artist) and bothered by my close relationship with her. He sank into a depression, during which he dressed almost exclusively in too-short sweatpants, a forest green terry cloth bathrobe, and worn Reebok high-tops.

When I was ten years old, my father moved out. My parents

went through a messy, combative, three-year divorce, after which my father popped in and out of my life; we grew apart and saw each other once a year until we stopped seeing each other entirely.

So this was what I knew of family, more or less. It was a broken unit, made up of obscure, semialienated people. All of my limited interactions with these people I was supposed to love were unfamiliar, uncomfortable. We were bound by blood or marriage, but I knew my mailman better than I knew them. In fact, my mailman lived next door, and I babysat his children.

෪

HOWEVER I FELT ABOUT FAMILIES, there was no avoiding the Crucianis. The Crucianis were monuments, institutions, the foundation of Emanuele's daily life. Like most Italian men, Emanuele had lived at home until I came along—an easy shift, if the wife who comes along takes over your mother's role. This was a culture of women who took care of men from birth to death, and of men who feigned incapability until they actually became incapable. Once, I watched a *nonna* bent over a cane, her swollen legs stuffed into beige panty hose, her feet balancing in orthopedic shoes, making her slow, steady way across the piazza, her spare arm clutching a pile of freshly starched and ironed dress shirts.

"She's been ironing her son's shirts for seventy-five years," a villager told me.

I was unable or unwilling to do what society dictates an Umbrian woman should do—including incessantly cleaning up after a man, killing chickens with my bare hands, and cooking lasagna and wild boar.

Men are easy with your deficiencies: They don't judge as harshly because usually they're not paying much attention. It was Emanuele's mother, Serenella, I worried about. I had seen her from a distance during that initial summer whirlwind romance. She peered out from behind the shrouded windows of her kitchen, frowning behind round glasses.

"You're living in *Roman Holiday*," she had observed dryly while I waited on the motorcycle in the driveway.

When Emanuele told the family that I was returning, Serenella told him she'd believe it when she saw it.

On the dreaded day of introduction, Emanuele and I pulled up to Casa Cruciani, a white two-story stucco structure located on a break in a winding hill, on a small flat plot on the way from the city of Todi to the center of Collelungo. A short drive of pale pebbles and a brick patio led to a house with a heavy wooden door, and small windows lined with flower boxes and protected by iron bars. All around grew rosebushes, tall grass, weeds, wildflowers, clover. A rusty outdoor table was spread with nuts, bolts, lighters, the discarded odds and ends of a workman's pocket. The parking area, stuffed with five small cars, was scattered with gas cans, plastic buckets, an elaborate water hose system, a pair of rubber boots, a hammer, a horseshoe. Two orange feral cats, each missing a chunk of ear, their long fur matted, sat curled but alert by the entrance.

Emanuele was already walking through the doorway, but I stood in the driveway. Would they accept me? Would they think me strange? This silent, urban American barging into their lives. Would they understand my understated yet sophisticated style, or would they just think I was a slob? Would they think me inept for not understanding the fundamentals of rural life?

My arrival elicited exactly no reaction.

"O, ciao," said Serenella, her voice hoarse from decades of cigarettes. She nodded her chin toward me and continued to stir a steaming pot on the stove. She stood in front of a bright yellow refrigerator in an alcove kitchen, open to the main room—a small woman, with the same large, hooded eyes as Emanuele. Her hair, which would go through a rainbow of color changes over the year, was dyed dirty blonde, cropped short, and permed, and she wore a long-sleeved cotton shirt, a pair of slacks, and beige leather mules. In a black-and-white photograph I would later see, she had been lush and delicate in her youth, curled up on a large rock, her shy handwriting scrawled on the back: *Per il mio marito, con tutto l'amore mio.* For my husband, with all my love—a memento for her other half during his army years. Now she was almost equally slender but slightly hunched, her face tired. She had a particular maternal strength, though. Touch her babies and she would happily slit your throat.

"Ciao," I returned meekly.

Emanuele's father, Fabio, sat on the couch, relaxed, legs stretched out, his mop of chestnut hair shining, his lips resting on the cigar that I would come to call *il sigaro infinito*. It seemed to be constantly burning. Though his brand of cigar, Antico Toscano, was available in town, he was convinced that each batch of cigars differed immensely from the next. He'd borrow a car from someone in his family (the only auto he owned was an ancient blue truck that once held up traffic for hours by stalling crosswise on the main through-way) and drive to every gas station and bar in a thirty-mile radius, sampling the same brand of cigar until he found the best batch. Since Fabio was cash poor, he could not afford to buy more than two packs at a time, or four if he was feeling flush, so he had to repeat the trek every other day. When the chosen store ran out of his batch, he began the ordeal anew.

"Ciao," I said.

"Ciao," Fabio said. He smiled, his brown skin creasing near his dark eyes, puffed on his cigar, and turned back to the blaring television. He sported a significant mustache. "Giustina," he said contentedly, getting himself used to my name, my presence.

"This is my brother Ettore," Emanuele said. Ettore leaned back on a chair near the fireplace, smoking a cigarette. He was all muscle and bone, not an ounce of fat on his long frame, thanks to weeks spent working construction and weekends spent splitting wood, riding horses, hunting birds, and fishing.

"He's also thin because he's really nervous," explained Emanuele.

Ettore's face was tanned and coarse, his blond hair sun-bleached and tangled. He wore camo pants and scuffed black leather work boots and a blue T-shirt that bore the image of the Warner Bros. Tasmanian Devil. He flashed me a grin. He was the skinny blond who had been attempting to mount the lightbulb at the bar the past summer—the one atop the ladder, shooting me lascivious looks.

"He makes love to many woman," Emanuele once reflected. "Maybe he must hit her on the head like a caveman, but he gets the woman."

Ettore was a study in contrasts: He was a great and helpful friend, a constant brother and son, generous to those he loved, and handy in the field. He was an expert outdoorsman, and he worked long days performing hard physical labor without complaint. He adored all children. He loved babies and toddlers and preteens; he took them on his horse, balanced them on his shoulders, tickled them. On the other hand, he had no regard for animals. Once, when I discovered a dead cat in the backyard, Emanuele nonchalantly blamed Ettore.

"If you saw a dead cat, Ettore probably killed it," he said.

"Why?"

"Because the savage cats like to hunt a type of savage chicken," Emanuele said. "Ettore also likes to hunt the savage chicken."

Ettore loved his girlfriend, Marta, an earthy twenty-five-year-old with a nest of black curls and an athletic build. He had kept her as his own from the time she was fifteen. At the same time, Ettore was partial to partying at far-off clubs and engaging in intimate relations with other women.

When he was seven years old, he had despised his schoolteacher, whom he considered a bossy old hag. During that particular year, the schoolteacher's husband had drowned in a fishing accident. In the months following the man's death, little Ettore spent his art lessons gleefully drawing the same image with his bright crayons: a fishing pole, a wave, and a tombstone.

"Hello, Joo-stine," Ettore said.

"And this, Paolo." Paolo was trim and tidy, age twenty-two. His hair was painstakingly gelled into a mini-hawk, and a wash of pimples spread across his forehead. He wore expensive clothes, each and every detail labeled, down to his sneakers, which were silver and embossed with rhinestone studs spelling out the popular brand name of their maker: RICH. Paolo was a geometer, a soccer player, college educated and even tempered. He and his long-term girlfriend, Cassandra, were impeccably coordinated (if she wore a magenta skirt, he wore a magenta shirt) and on some weekends borrowed her father's yellow convertible to zip through the countryside. Paolo slipped in and out of the house unnoticed most of the time, made his bed, kept his room neat, and rarely smoked.

"Nice to meet you," he said bashfully, in English.

Emanuele and I sat on the couch and joined Fabio in watching the news delivered by breathless Italian female broadcasters with kohl-rimmed eyes, long, lustrous hair, and brightly colored, complicated jackets. I couldn't understand many of the words, but the intonation, I noted, was far more drastic than that on American news, where our covered-up, bullet-headed journalists try to appear objective. For the Italians, each story was its own unique drama, and they, the narrators, charged with doing that drama justice. When children suffered, the newsmen and -women gave it their all, raising their voices, alternating between outrage, sadness, and shock. "Il piccolo Tommaso," they began. The newspapers rang out: *What Monster Killed Little Tommy?* For me, it was an early harbinger of the Italian obsession with children. Children, above and beyond all else, were to be worshipped and adored, kissed, coddled, admired, beloved, and allowed to do whatever they wanted whenever they wanted, while adults sat around chuckling at the pure cuteness.

Fabio himself was mostly obsessed with Francesco, his daughter's butterball of a smiling baby. Francesco, Fabio theorized, was the world's happiest baby because he was "molto amato." Much loved. Much-loved babies knew it, Fabio said. They knew they were adored, and so they became ever happier and thereby ever more adorable. Francesco generally arrived toted by his cherubic, bespectacled mother, Alessandra, the family's A+ student and an architect. She had married a chef, and they lived together in a simple, small house a few towns away. Francesco, at six months, was the first grandchild, the first nephew, and his entrance to the house that evening caused the entire Cruciani family to more or less fall prostrate. He was their soft and tiny god.

"Franci," they squealed. "Franci," they cooed. He was passed around.

"Bucala bucala bucala," Fabio sang to him. "Bucala bucala bucala," and Franci's entire face lit up, his monotoothed grin growing wider until he burst into laughter and the entire room rejoiced. I was going to have to learn to adore babies. Babies: those little saliva vehicles, those flailing, wailing, gummy-mouthed, fleshy creatures.

"È molto bello," I said expectantly, and the family nodded at me approvingly and returned their focus to Franci.

SO THIS WAS A FAMILY, and I was part of it. I was part of it immediately. My presence was understood as something unremarkable, something factual. Giustina is part of this family. *È così.* The first two nights, I was forbidden from helping with the dishes. I was a guest; guests drink a *caffè* and go home. On the third night, I forced myself into the kitchen, fiddled with the faulty faucet, and began to scrub. And from then on, I was a substitute Cruciani. I was Zia Giustina to Francesco, just another adult child for whom to make some spaghetti. That's how it seemed.

In reality, the Crucianis' open home was indicative of their extreme courtesy. I knew that I had been accepted as all serious significant others had: totally and completely, until the romantic relationship ruptured. Then, I'd be on my own, which was the nature of the family, I supposed: You are either forever in or forever on the precipice of being banished.

"O, MA" ECHOED THROUGH CASA Cruciani.

"O, Ma," heavy and deep, from the upstairs bedroom or the downstairs bathroom.

"O, Ma, where are my pants, where is my hat, where is the shampoo?"

"In the drawer, on the floor, under the sink," Serenella yelled at the top of her lungs.

"O, Ma, can you fix my shirt?"

"O, Ma, clean these shoes."

"O, Ma, this meat is too salty."

"O, Ma, I have a headache." Or "O, Ma, give me a cigarette."

Serenella was the extrastrength superglue that held the family together, that ruled the house, and that slaved for all four of her grown children, and perhaps the biggest feat of all, for Fabio. She possessed an internal wellspring of power and could cook a four-course meal in twenty minutes, fix an electrical outlet, refinish a cabinet, raise a prizewinning rose garden. She worked days cleaning the expansive castle of an American art dealer and spent her nights feeding and cleaning up after her grown brood.

Serenella mended the shirt, buffed the shoes. She cooked the meals as they liked them (more meat, less green) and handed over ibuprofen, cigarettes, and sometimes money. She ironed shirts, hung up sheets, and mopped the floor. The boys stomped around in their muddy boots, back and forth across the glossy terra-cotta tiles, day in and day out, and she followed absently with a mop.

"Mi fa impazzire," I blurted out after watching a ten-minute session of this repeat cleaning. "How many times do you do this?"

She looked at me with the compassionate pity reserved for the naive. "Oh, sometimes in the winter I mop the floor eight times a day," she said.

"O, Serenell—" Fabio hollered from the bedroom. "Where are my socks?"

"His socks have been in the same place for thirty years," Serenella said. "Che stupido." Then she went to get Fabio his socks.

Serenella took a casual liking to me. She was wildly, inexplicably tolerant. Had the situation been reversed, I would not have been so open-minded. During the evenings when Emanuele played poker at the bar and Fabio went to bed, Serenella and I sat in front of *Capri,* an evening soap opera. We had located a channel that showed English subtitles, so we perched in front of the fire, rapt, rooting for Angela, the good, poor blonde, and cursing rich, dark Vittoria. I stumbled with my Italian, pronouncing words incorrectly and drawing out my sentences, but Serenella hardly seemed to notice. She ignored my mumbled apologies, and she replied long and fast as she pulled from her cigarette and knit or sewed.

"Piano, piano," I often interrupted to make her slow down.

Serenella was always mending clothes, polishing shoes, repairing furniture. But to relax, she liked to make lace by hand. As we watched *Capri,* she created a pattern of wooden and porcelain bobbins on a small, round pillow, wrapping thin ecru threads into a butterfly, or a series of flowers at the edge of a curtain.

"I can't cook a thing," I confessed, as Vittoria and Angela glared at each other in the kitchen of the hotel in which they were fighting over the same man. "In New York, I always ate out."

"Of course you don't know how to cook," Serenella said, matter-of-fact. "This isn't your world."

She was concerned for me. In her heart, I believe, she was sorry that I was alone in a strange land. Italians were never alone—to them, loneliness was the most unbearable sensation, solitude the most dreadful circumstance. When they drove to do errands in another town, they usually asked somebody to accompany them, *per fare compagnia.* Dinner for one was a tragedy that nobody should have to bear.

"Chi mangia solo crepa solo," they moaned. He who eats alone dies alone.

"I know what it's like to be a stranger," she told me on one of our evenings together. I was learning Italian mostly from her, since she knew no English other than an embarrassed, heavily accented "Would you like coffee or tea?" which she had learned because the American art dealer sometimes hired her on as a server at a dinner party. "When I was only twenty, Fabio and I moved forty miles away for his work. I didn't know even one person."

They had no car, and even if they had, Serenella refused to drive more than fifteen minutes in any direction. "I was completely *da sola,*" she said. "Just me and Fabio."

"Was he a good friend to you?" I asked.

"Ma, dai," she said, using the colloquial phrase for *come on.* "He is *Fabio.*"

FABIO: YOU COULD GIVE THE man a thriving shop selling cheap rice in a country on the brink of starvation and he'd run the place into the red in under four days. He was not diligent, ambitious, or cautious. He had trouble controlling fourteen sheep and could hardly change a lightbulb. And yet, you really had no choice but to adore him.

"Giustina, Giustina, Giustina," Fabio liked to mutter when he saw me.

Or, "Giusti-i-i-ina!"—an excited cry.

"*Mamma mia,* Giustina sure is an ugly name," he once said, and then smiled brightly.

"Really?" I asked.

Everyone at the dinner table nodded. "Bruttissimo."

Fabio carried a bucket full of oats, or a rake, or a piece of hose that he intended to jerry-rig to three other pieces of hose, which would constitute one extended hose that could water the garden or wash the horse. Fabio looked like a movie star playing a farmer, except for the authentic touch of toothlessness, which was hidden beneath his mustache.

"Ever since the army, he's been traumatized by toothpaste," Emanuele explained one day. "They put it in his pillowcase to tease him, and now he gets sick from the smell."

"What about your mother? Doesn't she demand that he take care of his teeth?" I asked.

"She has given up." Meanwhile, Serenella swept the floor as Fabio raised his feet.

"Non è buono per niente," she muttered. Good for nothing.

"Vero," he said happily.

Fabio stood six feet tall but slouched slightly and was never in a rush to get anywhere, oblivious, or impervious, to the passing of time. His hair was so lustrous, he could have been a mature, rugged male model on the side of the Just For Men hair dye box.

"But why is your hair so fabulous?" I asked one evening at dinner. None of his three sons had hair anything like it—Ettore had strawlike blond curls, Emanuele's brown locks were waning, and Paolo's hair had been shorn into a harsh buzz cut.

"Because you can only wash once a week," Fabio declared. "And stress. You cannot stress."

"It's true," his father, Renato, said. Renato, at eighty, also sported a full head of shiny salt-and-pepper hair, as well as a thick gray mustache. "Thirty years ago, when I had a bad job and was always worried, I lost all of my hair. I went to the doctor and said, 'What is happening?' And the doctor said, 'If you want your hair back, you must quit your job.'"

"He was *completely* bald," Serenella said.

"I left the job," Renato said. "Within two months, I had my hair back."

"Infatti," Fabio said. "You must avoid stress at all costs." Serenella, her back sore from a fourteen-hour day, glared at him. "Also for the skin, it's important to not shower more than once a week," he added.

"My father is very proud that he only showers once a week," Emanuele said. "He should probably be ashamed, but he is proud."

"It *is* true that you work closely with sheep every day," I said.

"Eh . . . beh," Fabio bleated. He cut himself a hunk of *parmigiano* and a slice of soft, browned pear, and leaned back in his chair at the head of the table. "Life is not as dirty as you think."

Eh . . . beh was Fabio's favorite phrase. It summed up his philosophy and might have been thinly translated as "Oh well. . . . God will handle it."

Beh, Fabio had set up a small firewood business when he retired from his decades as a schoolteacher for special education students. *Beh,* he blew his pension by taking out loans he couldn't pay back, by refusing to keep the books, by paying his lone Macedonian employee more than he made in profit. *Beh,* Emanuele and Ettore had worked for years to gain the house back from bank ownership, but to no avail.

"There is nothing more evil than an Italian bank," Emanuele told me. They were sloppy, corrupt institutions with unethical

borrowing practices. I believed it, too. Italy seemed a country built
on nepotism, on getting the most for you and yours, damn the others, and there was very little effective oversight to counteract that
approach. If you had enough money, you could buy yourself out of
jail, out of service, out of any sort of trouble. If you did not, you were
up the creek, paddle free.

While Alessandra worked on her master's in architecture at the
Università di Roma and Paolo finished high school and studied to
become a geometer, Emanuele and Ettore took up the family cause
and worked days in the deep forest, cutting down pine trees, splitting logs, aging the pieces in the open air, bundling them, delivering
them, and running from bank to bank, paying off borrowed money
with more borrowed money, until everything the family had ever
owned belonged to the bank. Their house and land, which had been
Cruciani property for over a hundred years, were the bank's property now. They never paid more than the interest, which continued
to accumulate. Emanuele, who had once wanted to be a teacher of
literature, left college after one year to return and help save his
father's business.

Ettore, on the other hand, had never been much of a student.
Decades earlier, on a school day, Serenella had been walking down a
back road when she had seen, poking out from under a bush, a pair
of small sneakers. She bent down and found five-year-old Ettore sitting there, a skinny banged-up thing with a blond bowl cut, eating
the lunch she had packed for him. "Playing hooky in first grade,"
Emanuele had told me.

Still, Ettore had hoped to make some cash by joining a building crew and instead was stuck chopping wood for no more than
room and board to pay off his father's debt.

Ettore and Emanuele were also offered up to military service.
In Italy, until 2005, army service was compulsory for two out of
three sons in a family. Paolo had been spared, but Ettore and

Emanuele had been shipped off for a year each to serve as ambulance medics and firemen in faraway provinces for a stipend of about nine hundred dollars per month. But neither Ettore nor Emanuele held anything against Paolo. They were relieved that he alone had been absolved. When Fabio asked Paolo for some money, as he did every other month, Emanuele and Ettore intervened.

"You've ruined our credit," they said. "Don't you dare touch Paolo's."

Fabio looked pained. He still sold firewood, and he often did not have enough to pay the worker who helped him haul the product. If Ettore or Emanuele had some extra, they'd loan it to Fabio. If not, Fabio began his calm stroll to his brother's to ask for a buck. When a small parcel of land that he had long been using to graze his sheep opened up for sale, Fabio grew dejected. The land, which belonged to a distant cousin, had once belonged to Fabio's grandfather. He needed it. Emanuele and Ettore dutifully handed over whatever meager savings they had, even though the land, too, would eventually belong to the bank, which now deducted a monthly fee from Fabio's pension checks.

"Why bother helping him with that land?" I asked Emanuele.

"Because he needs that land," Emanuele said, "or his heart will break."

WHILE ALESSANDRA AND PAOLO WORKED at shiny architecture firms, Emanuele trimmed olive trees at his English boss's estate and Ettore bounced from job to job, as an underpaid construction worker and later as a well-compensated metalworker for his uncle. But nobody was mad or jealous, as far as I could tell. Even Serenella, who spent her days scrubbing toilets, dusting the antique tables in the castle, and laundering the American art collector's dirty clothes, didn't seem resentful. She didn't understand the fuss he made over dinner parties, and often wondered aloud why the wealthy spent a week preparing for a supper, when she could make a meal for ten in under thirty minutes, using ingredients from her cabinets and garden. She was puzzled at the apparent senselessness of the lifestyle: Why buy expensive, exotic flower arrangements when you have a field of buttercups and bluebells just outside your door?

Italy wasn't a land of dreams and ambitions, not like America. Italians were attached to what was theirs, not longing for what might someday be theirs. If, for example, your father was not a *carabiniere,* or policeman, you would have a hard time becoming a *carabiniere.* If your father worked at a factory, you would have a job waiting at a factory. If your father was a wealthy lawyer, you might become a wealthy lawyer. More or less, the class system was set in place, and Italian children were not brought up to an adult chorus chirping, "What do you want to do?" The world was not open to them in that way—an endless choice of professions, all of them seeking someone new and better. There was little room for the children of a lumberjack to nurse wild ambitions. Because they knew that this was the deal from the get-go, Italians were not crushed when their lofty fantasies failed to materialize. That they did not manage to get jobs in banks was of no great consequence to Ettore or Emanuele, both of whom looked like shifty, uncomfortable twelve-year-olds when they had to wear their suits anyway.

WHEN FRANCESCO WAS NOT AT Casa Cruciani, Fabio drove for twenty minutes just to hold him for an hour. He didn't know how to feed the baby or change his diapers, and could hardly calm him (for that, Serenella swooped in), but he wanted to hold him, to say, "Bucala bucala bucala." If his daughter and her husband took Francesco to the lake for a week, Fabio drove to their house before they returned home and started a fire to warm the place.

When I left for a week, Fabio's eyes welled up with tears.

"Giustina, you must come back soon," he said, slumped in his seat.

"Hey, *stupido*, she's going away for only a week," Serenella said.

It was humanly impossible to be angry at Fabio. You couldn't even dislike him. Fabio was *pace:* peace, personified.

"My mother can be crude," Emanuele once admitted. "But my father is somehow gracious." *Un gran galantuomo,* Fabio.

"How can I hate him?" Emanuele asked. "When we were children, we never wanted anything. Even when my parents had no money, they found a way for us to go on every school trip, to always have new clothes. He gave us everything he could."

Fabio had spent decades patiently teaching special education classes. He wore a rosary around his neck. He took his weekly bath on Sundays, before Mass. He ate his dinner slowly, savoring it, sitting in his wooden chair at the head of the table long after everyone else had sunk into their places on the couch. When he drove, he listened to Catholic radio; he fell asleep to it, too, to classical music or the rhythmic Hail Mary played on repeat. *Ave Maria, gratia plena, Dominus tecum, virgo serena . . .*

But Fabio didn't broadcast his God. He didn't bring the family with him to church. He didn't pass judgment on others. His expression was fixed in a casual smile, and when he had something, anything, he gave it away, which was partially why he had nothing. He could not bear life without his children, and secretly invited Emanuele and me to move in with him and Serenella.

"Come live with us," he whispered. "You can stay upstairs and everything is free. No rent, you don't pay heat, good food."

Fabio admitted freely that he was a sucker for *le bestie*. Indeed, as long as a creature's heart beat, Fabio could not ignore it. Though the people of Collelungo, and of most farm communities, were rough with and matter-of-fact about their future meat, Fabio was almost paternal. Once, an older ewe broke her leg, and Fabio was alone on the farm. Though a more pragmatic person would have shot the casualty—you really can't cure an injured, elderly farm animal—Fabio placed her shin in a crudely constructed splint. The sheep looked preposterous, hobbling around her shed, and she eventually died. The days leading up to her inevitable death tortured Fabio, who paced, brow furrowed.

"I should have just killed her," he said helplessly. "Now she suffers!"

FABIO HAD THEORIES, PRECIOUS THEORIES, about everything.

"The young must eat a lot of pork," he said.

"Don't feed a child eggs unless you want to kill it," he asserted.

"Redheads cannot be trusted."

"You should stop reading so much," he told me whenever I sat with a book. "The more you know, the more dissatisfied you are."

"Don't you read?"

"Io? Solo la Bibbia," he said. Only the Bible.

When I brought out a small sheet of paper used to blot oil from the face, the family regarded me curiously.

"What's that?" Serenella asked.

I pressed it on my nose and took it off, showing her the mark of oil on the paper. Then I gave her one, which she pressed against her nose. People around the world may have appreciated the beauty of a matte face, but Fabio was unimpressed.

"You know why you have oil on your face?" he asked. "Because you *need* oil on your face!"

Later, I gave Serenella an expensive mud mask, which she wore while vacuuming when Fabio was not around.

Once, as we watched a news program, Fabio muttered that the reason Italy was such a political mess was because they did not have a George W. Bush in charge.

"Ma che scherzi?" I asked. Are you kidding?

"Bush, Berlusconi, they are *leaders*," Fabio said, puffing on *il sigaro infinito*.

I looked around the room, everyone shaking their heads. The Italian government had gone through several collapses during my time there. "We're the next Argentina," Emanuele had taken to saying, so fragile and unbalanced were the economic and political systems. Silvio Berlusconi, the corrupt Milanese media magnate, billionaire business mogul, and on-and-off prime minister, was generally disliked by the liberal working poor, who knew he wasn't out for their interests. The Crucianis tended to support the messier, liberal candidates like Romano Prodi, the newly elected prime minister whose mismanaged government imploded as soon as he took office.

"Fabio likes Berlusconi?" I asked nobody in particular.

"My father is a mystery," Alessandra said.

"We all used to argue with him about politics over dinner," Emanuele said. "But then when Paolo was little, he began to cry about the fighting, so we don't talk about it anymore."

Serenella, perched on a sofa arm, took a drag of her long cigarette. "Sì!" she raised her voice, motioning at Fabio, who was gazing into the distance and puffing on his *sigaro*. "This poor farmer without a lira to his name is for Berlusconi."

"Ma perché? Perché?" I asked Fabio.

"Eh . . . beh," he shrugged.

"Beh!" Serenella said. A communal *beh* swept the room, and everyone returned to what they had been doing.

For the Crucianis, parents and siblings were not creatures to be analyzed in relation to each other; no, they just *were*. No questions asked about their neuroses, personalities, hopes, dreams, desires, disappointments, failures. When Ettore—volatile, violent Ettore—beat someone up, the family responded with no more than, at the most, a pained shrug. That was just Ettore. *È così*, he's like that. You could throw a pitcher of wine at the couch or go into debt or kick an innocent bystander's ass, and everyone would nod. The family existed as the most solid unit; since nothing was evaluated and everything was accepted, they were not vulnerable to rupture.

Before I had returned to Collelungo, I had figured that I could be fitted effortlessly into Emanuele's life. But I now realized that I tended to experience a spontaneous panic when dropped into the middle of a group of close friends, or a family. It was a sensation comparable only to the pang of homesickness I would feel as a child on the school bus, staring out the window, rolling slowly away from my white house on the small hill, and then suddenly gripped with a sharp longing for my mother that nearly made me cry. I would steel myself against my loneliness, and it would soon subside. I had the same reaction once in a while when I sat with a group of people who were already close with one another. Previously, I'd been puzzled by my feelings and had responded by asserting how little I cared about inclusion. Now I think that assertion belied a certain wistfulness, the potent desire to be one of them, a permanent fixture, rather than a fleeting figure.

⟋⟍

DESPITE MY FEAR, I WAS at home with the Crucianis. Despite the language gap, the cultural abyss, the novelty of our relationship, after only two weeks with them, when I pulled up in front of their house for dinner, I felt the cozy sensation of homecoming. My presence was understood as unremarkable. *È così*. She's tall, doesn't understand much, can't cook meatballs, is frightened of the sheep. *Eh . . . beh.*

I ate with them, watched TV with them, napped on their couches, herded their sheep. When my pants tore, Serenella fixed them. When my stomach hurt, Fabio served me *la camomilla.* More *parmigiano* was provided for me, because I liked a lot on my spaghetti. More wood on the fire when I was cold. I swept their living room after dinner, brushing the mounds of bread crumbs out the door for the orange ferals to pick at. I dusted the bookshelves, laid out the silverware. Here, there were no complex rituals, no clubs closed to the public, no family secrets, no whispered arguments in the privacy of a bedroom. No outsiders, no insiders. The door was open—park, enter, eat a piece of bread, a slice of prosciutto. These were not precious, private nests, but open spaces. What happened in them happened in full view of everyone.

I SAW THIS EVIDENCED ONE national holiday, just after my arrival. Italy seemed to have hundreds of such days, mostly for reasons unknown to the population, during which the entire country shut down and Italians exercised their right to shirk work. Early that morning, I walked down the steep hill, from the top of which I could see the rusty slopes heading to Todi. At the bottom, I turned into the white driveway and popped my head into Casa Cruciani. Fabio was downing his second espresso of the day. Alessandra— who, with the baby, spent the night when her husband worked until two or three in the morning at his restaurant—was emerging from her room in her pajamas and fixing herself a breakfast of *caffè latte* and biscuits.

Mornings in the house were typically quiet and warm, the terracotta floor sun-dappled, a fire going, two just-delivered loaves of bread on the table. But on that day, the place was in disarray—piles of dirty pots and pans were stacked in the kitchen, Francesco's toys strewn on the floor, a layer of grime coating everything. Meanwhile, Fabio and Alessandra sat on the couch, looking paler than usual, and tried to entertain Francesco, who had begun to cry. They weren't great at accomplishing things, the father-daughter duo. They were similar: slow, deliberate, thoughtful. Where was Serenella?

"La mamma sta male," Alessandra explained. Serenella was bedridden with the flu.

The kitchen was covered in dirty dishes, and I recognized that I should clean up. But it was tricky: Would Alessandra be somehow offended? Could I just barge in at eight o'clock in the morning and take over? And frankly, I didn't want to spend an hour cleaning their house. I backed out, smiling.

For that holiday lunch, Emanuele and I went to Nonna Ferrina's house with the other cousins. Nonna Ferrina's house was a two-bedroom apartment nestled in the ancient town. In her entire life, Nonna Ferrina had never spent more than twenty lire for anything. She killed her own chickens and pigeons, smoked her own prosciutto, mashed her own grapes for wine, carted firewood for miles to stack it, saved rubber bands and wrapping paper, preserves, empty glass bottles, Tupperware, ropes, and any other useful item in her vast, cobweb-filled cellar. She wore muumuus purchased from a white van that drove through town once a month. It was packed with chintzy dresses and navigated by a Tunisian, who announced his arrival by blasting Italian dance music out of a loudspeaker attached to the top of the van. Nonna Ferrina had left Umbria only a handful of times—she was the remainder of the impoverished generation, and though she now was comfortable and her son Sauro ran a successful metalworking company, she lived low to the ground. She was round, bespectacled, and hard of hearing, and she shouted when she meant to speak. She was also permanently confused, about everything, and could be counted on to holler, "What? What happened?" in every conversation. Emanuele and

I shared a wall with her and her equally deaf husband, Nonno Marcello, and we could hear the television through the plaster.

Nonna Ferrina had given us a giant green plant for good luck when we'd moved in. (It promptly turned brown.) She brought us hard *crostata* pastry with fig jam and invited us to dinner at least once a week. She offered me espresso whenever she saw me. One day, after I complimented her homemade pasta, she arrived at my door, a gauzy scarf wrapped around her head, bearing tagliatelle laid out delicately on a gold piece of cardboard.

Once I was sitting on a small bench by the city walls and Nonno Marcello was standing outside of a garage he rented for his car and additional items that couldn't fit in the cellar. He appeared to be waving at me, and so I waved back, on and on for almost five minutes, as he looked increasingly frustrated and waved harder. I didn't understand anything he said at the beginning, and later on, even when I did speak the language, he and his wife became accustomed to staring at me with silent smiles before turning to Emanuele and beginning, "Tell Giustina . . ." Eventually, it occurred to me that Marcello was motioning me to come to him, which I had misinterpreted because instead of making the American gesture—which looks like you are pulling someone in with your hand, palm toward the sky—he was making the Italian gesture—which looks like you are pulling something down. I had misunderstood it to be a bizarre attempt at waving. When I finally approached, he hustled me into the garage, took out a plastic bag, and began to fill it to the brim with tomatoes from his garden and eggs from his chickens. More, more, more: He weighed me down with offerings and sent me off, all without a word.

On the holiday, Ferrina had prepared *lasagna bianca:* sheets of fresh homemade pasta, creamy béchamel sauce, meat ragout, sliced mushrooms, and *parmigiano.* She cut us slices that seemed to weigh in at a pound each and poured us her fizzy, tangy homemade red wine, which all the cousins seated at the table mixed immediately with water. Afterward, she presented the group—hunched over, as Collelungese seemed to do when they ate, shoveling lasagna into their mouths— with an oily stew of gamy chicken and tomato. When I could not manage it, having consumed so much lasagna, she began to fret.

"Giustina, Giustina, mangi poco. Mangi troppo poco," she said. "Mangia! Mangia!"

"This is *the* ultimate stereotype of an Italian grandmother," I told Emanuele, who looked at me, puzzled.

When we had finished lunch, we checked in at Casa Cruciani. Alessandra and Fabio had eaten a simple meal, and the dirty dishes were also piled on the table, along with crumbs. Emanuele and I sat down in front of the fire, where Fabio was now roasting chestnuts. I looked at the dishes again. But first, *una castagna,* a chestnut—fresh roasted, its meat crisp and sweet. Fabio buried them beneath the ashes and cooked them there for hours, and we uncovered them like jewels.

I took Francesco on my lap and began to peel a chestnut. Serenella emerged from the bedroom, still in her bathrobe, pallid, with dark circles under her eyes. She looked at the kitchen and sighed angrily. Then she went about the immense task, turning on the water and picking up the first pan.

Alessandra, whose temper was inversely proportional to the amount of sleep she got with Francesco around, snipped at her mother. "What? You want me to feel sorry for you?" she asked.

Serenella replied with equal venom, and the squabble escalated. Emanuele and Fabio and I sat watching from the couches, Francesco balanced on my lap, rapt upon seeing his mother and grandmother raise their voices. At first it was a distraction, an oddity, worth our attention. I didn't understand the words, which devolved into Umbrian dialectal drawl as the women got angrier. Their voices rose as they grew more combative. Fabio tilted his head from his vantage point on the couch. And then suddenly, Alessandra, gentle, soft-spoken

Alessandra, erupted, letting out a bellow from the gut. I clutched Francesco to my chest as she took the tablecloth in two hands and pulled with all her might, sending plates and glasses to the floor, penne sticking to the wall. She then stomped to the counter, grabbed the jug of wine, and threw it against the tiles, where it shattered, sending blood red liquid and glass flying. In tears, she ran through the house, out the rickety garage door, breaking it from its hinges, and threw herself on the dusty ground by the road.

I looked about, shell-shocked. Hadn't they seen me there? Weren't non–family members prohibited from witnessing nervous breakdowns? Emanuele, who seemed mildly concerned, followed his sister outside. Serenella was muttering to herself. I was not in Connecticut anymore.

"You should have shut up," Fabio said.

"*You* should shut up," Serenella said. She began to sweep the glass.

I pointed impotently at the stained couch, and Serenella shrugged. I kept Francesco balanced on my hip.

"Bucala bucala?" I said. He giggled. "Bucala," I said again. Fabio took the baby from me, and I searched silently for a broom.

While I swept the floor, Alessandra returned, her eyes puffy and cheeks wet with tears. She took Francesco from her father, placed him in her car, and drove off.

"She's really tired," Emanuele said, sinking into the couch and lighting a cigarette. "And Ma, you should have kept your mouth shut."

"What did she say?" I asked him, in English.

"She say my sister is no good as a mother," Emanuele said. "She say my sister cannot do this job. My sister say that my mother cannot care for Francesco anymore then."

Serenella had a point, though it may not have warranted such destruction: Alessandra wasn't capable like Serenella. When Emanuele was young, Serenella had cleaned houses with Alessandra balanced on her hip, Emanuele nearby, entertaining himself in a cardboard box. She'd held a job and raised four children on the brink of poverty, washing and sewing clothing, fixing three excellent meals a day, shopping, cleaning. Meanwhile, Alessandra, while a capable architect and the smartest and best-educated member of the family, was a miserable multitasker. It turned out that she had intended to wash the dishes but had been unable to acquire the necessary rubber gloves to protect her sensitive skin.

Serenella was now back to scrubbing two days' worth of cooking grease from her kitchen. She was dressed in a bathrobe, mumbling under her breath. Fabio wandered off to check his sheep.

Later that evening, I asked Emanuele what would happen after such an argument.

"I predict that within a day, everything will be normal again," he said.

The next day, I walked through the heavy doors and into the living room, to find Francesco bouncing up and down on Fabio's lap on the wine-speckled couch. Alessandra and Serenella cooked together in the kitchen, neither jolly nor dour. Alessandra threw me a shy hello.

"That was fast," I remarked to Emanuele.

He nodded absently. "All of us always come back," he said.

ALL KNOWLEDGE, THE TOTALITY
OF ALL QUESTIONS AND ALL ANSWERS,
IS CONTAINED IN THE DOG.

—FRANZ KAFKA

I WAS NEVER A SOCIAL butterfly or the life of the party. Most of
the time I wasn't even in attendance at the party. I was usually busy
pretending to be at another party while I in fact sat at home in
my pajamas with deep conditioner on my hair, watching forensics reality shows, eating take-out Vietnamese noodles, and reading melancholy Israeli poetry. Though this routine was voluntary and strangely
pleasant, it meant that I was often quite lonely, a state that did not
improve as I became increasingly familiar with both the techniques
used in a standard autopsy and Yehuda Amichai's collection of pro-
foundly sorrowful work. My loneliness was a choice, but I didn't know
that there was an alternative for quite some time. I did not require
many friends and would never be able to flit around gatherings—since
that involved being blessed with a higher tolerance for people and,
when you are young, a more developed affinity for beer and Jell-O
shots—but I required more than I had admitted to myself.

When I left Brooklyn for Collelungo, I wanted to escape the competitive grind and the dirty streets, but I wanted most of all to escape the inevitable, omnipresent solitude of New York City, where even the most popular and famous are often anonymous, lost in the shadows of the buildings and the crowds. Surrounded by so many stimuli, I felt my isolation magnified.

In hindsight, it's obvious that moving from America's most populous urban center into a foreign farming village where you don't speak the language to live with a man you've known for only three weeks might increase a general sense of alienation. But, as with most relationships heavy on sexual chemistry and exotic romance, my vision got cloudy. *Del senno di poi son piene le fosse,* the Italians say: Graves are filled with after-the-fact wisdom.

Everything snapped back into focus early in my stay, and I saw that I could not remain with Emanuele. I would have liked to spend every waking moment sitting beside him, tapping away at my computer. For someone who thought of herself as a lone wolf, I was content to sit in the passenger seat of Emanuele's Twingo and be carted about, listening to Vecchioni singing love songs that referred to *la gioia del tuo culo e del tuo cuore:* the joy of your ass and your heart.

For a long time, without even knowing it, I had envisioned a perfect, fictional love in which two people came together, forever devoted only to one another. This idea of love caused a chain of letdowns, what with it being unhealthy and unrealistic. In this love that I dreamed of, the two pieces operate as a whole. Where I walk, you follow. When I lie down, you curl up beside me. If I leave, you stand by the door, awaiting my return. When we part, I feel like a portion of me is missing. When we're together, our bodies always touch. When you run, I watch you with admiration. When I read, you place your head on my knee.

When I think about it now, this grand love for which I toured the earth could be found most easily not between a man and a woman but between a doting owner and her loyal dog. That would account for a lot.

THERE IS A POINT EARLY on in every doomed relationship, a point at which one or both people recognize, in a passing moment of lucidity, that they are not meant for one another. Two people are sitting on a windblown beach somewhere on the Mediterranean. One looks upon the crashing green surf, breathes in deeply, and smiles, shocked silent by the astounding raw beauty, and right then, the other person launches into a speech about how he was cheated out of a couple of francs by that asshole at the street market an hour ago, and how he has half a mind to go back there and give that cheater what he has coming. The person breathing deeply fixes the ranter with her eyes and sees their love hurtling toward inevitable ruination. Some people, those who look their lives squarely in the face, extricate themselves immediately from these relationships. Others take some time. And a bunch get hitched anyway.

One October day, Emanuele left me in our chilly stone apartment to work on the businessman's book while he went to hunt birds in the fields with his cousin Flavio. He was setting a precedent, the same one he'd been setting from the moment I'd landed: cards at the bar, fishing trips, solo drives to visit Francesco. He was into community; I was into privacy. When I hoped to stay home with him alone, he resisted me. In turn, when he asked me to join him on his adventures—really, to sit by his side in the basement of the bar or travel with him to the mulch store—I resisted him.

That autumn day, he wore worn green pants and brown leather boots, and he looked as handsome as ever. He kissed me hard. He called me *amore*. Then he left me alone, and I watched him saunter to the car and drive out of the stone town, flinging the car around the sharp corner. As the little blue two-door disappeared, I felt a pang of woeful certainty: We would not last. Emanuele wanted to be willfully free and untethered to the fluid confines of a domestic partnership. I wanted to be bound; I wanted us to need only each other, to the exclusion of all else. I wanted to repeat those days in the room in Morruzze forever, and he wanted to live a pretty unchanged, casual life, hanging out in Collelungo with Valerio and Gianmaria and Gianluca. Since neither desire is especially evolved, it followed that neither of us was particularly well suited for any sort of enduring relationship—especially an enduring relationship with each other. It would probably be a cycle of disappointments and frustrations, punctuated by moments of passion and tenderness, during which we would whisper dramatically, "Ti amo tantissimo."

However, I had left Brooklyn in a flurry, with such conviction and commitment. It would have been an embarrassment to admit that my romantic experiment had failed immediately, to slink off back to the outer borough after just thirty days, to reclaim my apartment and resume my old life, which, in its final weeks, had involved the quotidian highlight of one pressed mushroom empanada, ordered from the deli on the corner. Sometimes with a black cherry soda.

More important, I had a keen but hazy sensation, only vaguely formed, that my time in Italy was not supposed to end so quickly, that I was not nearly finished with Collelungo, even if I did not believe that Emanuele and I were meant to be. So the moment that I came to my realization, I tried my best to bury it in the back of my brain and to march forward in my love affair. I couldn't find it within myself to leave. If I had described the relationship to any woman who wished me well, she would have rightfully advised me to book it out of there. I should be looking for appropriate men and pushing my life forward in an acceptable way, not waiting for a man I was just getting to know to return from hunting. But I was convinced that I was just getting started in Collelungo—though for what, I could not yet say.

IN THE EARLY DAYS, WHILE Emanuele aimed his shotgun up at the *uccelli* circling above the pastures, I often wandered around town just before lunch, when the local families had burrowed into their homes, and the streets went silent. I walked down Via Todi in the still air and felt that I had stepped into a land that time forgot. Advances that dictated the modern world were absent from the streets—no sleek cars or contemporary houses, no bright green lawns, no satellite dishes. The back fields had been plowed by the farmers living in adjacent houses; the front plots were gardens full of ancient mauve rosebushes. Every house was surrounded by a gated fence, whether ornamental or protective, even though most of the front doors were never locked. The homes were fortresses, at least symbolically, and shrines to the families that lived within them. At that hour, when the streets were empty, it was an untouched village. And in some ways, even when the workday resumed, it remained so.

One afternoon, I headed down to the Cruciani farm, over Via Todi's steep drop. I was thinking mainly about my education's failure to provide me with any tools with which to face this specific situation. I was thinking that school had not prepared me to be stuck in a two-hundred-person town, much as school had not prepared me for the main challenges of relatively privileged adult life: interpersonal dynamics, credit card debt, dashed hopes, injustices, and a load of professional and personal rejection. School had made it seem as if there were some magical, universal trajectory that we would all be swept along, and that at the end lay a series of fixed, comfortable landing pads from which we could take our pick. I remembered a conversation I'd had with my mother during my freshman year in college. I was nineteen years old.

"You know, life never smooths out," she said after I complained about some difficulty I had faced. "Some times are better and some are worse, but it's not as though you will ever be entirely free of struggle."

It seemed to be a terrible thing she'd just said to me—offensive, a lie, proof only that she had experienced an individual disappointment that she had erroneously interpreted as universal. I had been laboring under the impression that I was working past difficulties and toward an easy future. I had envisioned a climb to a plateau, not an infinite hike. The plateau seemed far preferable, and so I rejected her assertion.

"Maybe for you," I hissed. "But not for me."

I figured that I had ultimate control over my life. I could steer it to a comfortable place and park there. I would not continue driving, taking wrong turns, hitting road bumps, crashing, burning, and getting back up again, scratched and battered.

Now, if my mother were that sort of person, she could have said, "I told you so."

I turned into the crushed-stone driveway, passed the rickety table, and pressed on the heavy oak door. After a string of robberies (*by Albanians,* the locals insisted. *By Macedonians. By Romanians. By Russians! But not by us!*) in town, the Crucianis had taken to locking their door. Nobody was home for lunch yet—Serenella usually sped through the door at 1:05 and whipped up a hearty, balanced meal by 1:20. I decided to explore the grounds.

First, I headed down the small incline that brought me to the level of the barn. The barn was long and ramshackle, the ground surrounding the main path covered in old tires, chairs, metal poles, foam pads, lumps of shaved wool, broken glass. These things were never thrown away, but were rather saved, in a haphazard style, and occasionally used years later to construct new hovels or boxes, or to patch holes, or to support cars.

The building itself had been constructed in steps by Fabio and *i figli.* There had been, initially, only a deep, freestanding wine cellar, filled with several wooden barrels and at least a million gnats. There, Fabio brewed his homemade wine every year and filled jugs with the purple stuff. When money came in, a space was added onto the cellar. Ettore, Emanuele, and Fabio, as well as the entire population of Collelungo, were either amateur or professional construction workers, some with more stringent specifications than others. The Cruciani family was not concerned with aesthetic technicalities like constructing a uniform building; thus, the barn stretched unevenly for about fifty yards. A feed-and-water room, made of hand-poured concrete, had been soldered onto the cellar, followed by a wooden sleeping area for the sheep, then two brick-and-mortar storage rooms rented by a Roman actress who claimed that the family had lost two of her chaise longues and thus refused to pay while maintaining the spaces (Fabio received the news with a shrug and allowed her to stay on for years), and a cement area used to house a massive pile of rotting potatoes that were picked through, peeled, and cooked in the ever-simmering pot of *minestra*. The structure was finished off by a high-ceilinged studio hung thick with spiderwebs, where Daisy the Arabian mare lived, surrounded by tool tables.

The barn stood at the peak of a series of small hills that led to an open meadow in which Fabio's fourteen scraggly sheep grazed. The meadow was bordered by thick forest and speckled with a neighbor's olive trees. I had taken a few steps out to gaze upon it when I was distracted by a flash of white to my right. I had never been this far down before and had never seen what lay past Daisy's stall.

A mess of wire fencing was attached to the horse barn and driven into the concrete wall to create a small pen. The fencing had ripped with wear and had been repaired with an old wire bed frame, which had been secured over a hole in the front, its legs sticking straight out, threatening to impale the eye of an unsuspecting passerby. The pen was set on a plot of stinking, tamped-down dirt beneath a fig tree. There were ancient animal turds and rotting fruit scattered across the ground. In the corner sat a wooden box with an unevenly cut rectangular opening, and two rusted pots balanced in the corner, one empty and one full of bright green, mossy sludge. At the very edge of the pen, pressing against the wire, stood a small, spotted dog.

"*What?*" I asked nobody in particular.

The dog had the deep chest and slender legs of a miniature greyhound and the delicate, round puppy face of a spaniel, but with a longer snout. It had wet brown eyes and a short white coat, spotted black, and its head and neck were entirely black, as if the dog had been dipped in a pot of ink. Its dry black nose twitched, taking in my scent. This was a worried dog, whose expression was at once hopeful and anxious. It wrinkled its forehead. Its tail, also black, as if the dog had been turned over and dipped once again in the pot of ink, wagged wanly, uncertainly, close to the body, a little series of back-and-forths. Standing a good three feet away, I could easily count its ribs. I moved closer and pushed my hand through the wire. The dog offered itself up for a pet, trembling slightly. Through the wire, I scratched its dusty chest.

"Don't worry," I said, my fingers touching its bony body. "We'll figure something out."

Then I marched up to the house, where the Crucianis were preparing lunch.

"Whose dog is that?" I demanded. Everyone looked at me, standing there, hands on my hips, my voice louder than they had ever heard it.

"What dog?" Alessandra asked. The room was hot with steam from the pasta, clouds of condensation sticking to the windows.

"The dog outside, in the cage, by Daisy," I said.

"Oh, *that* dog," Serenella said.

"Probably Ettore's dog," Alessandra said. "Probably for hunting."

"Does he *feed* his hunting dog?" I asked.

"It eats!" Fabio protested sheepishly.

"There's a dog down there," I said, turning to Emanuele. "You never said anything about a dog."

"That's true," Emanuele said, looking up from the TV. He wore ripped blue jeans and a navy T-shirt. He had pulled a gray cap low on his forehead, and his legs were resting on a chair. His beat-up construction boots lay toppled by the door.

"It's dying," I said.

"It's the breed!" Fabio insisted.

"The breed is so naturally skinny that it looks like it's about to die?" I glared at him. "*Vero, Fabio? Vero?*"

"She doesn't believe you," Alessandra informed her father. "Nice try."

"Someone gave that dog to Ettore a year ago," Emanuele reflected. "But Ettore hasn't gone hunting recently."

"Are you all mad?"

Serenella let out a chuckle.

"Giustina, Ettore has had about twenty dogs in his life," Alessandra said, picking Francesco up from his rocker. "I think maybe ten got sick and died. He shot two. Then, remember that dog he liked? But it bothered the neighbors, so they killed it."

I looked from face to face. Everyone nodded.

"There was also the time he got drunk on New Year's and in the morning, he wanted to go hunting, so he took the dog, but crashed the car," Emanuele added. "The dog seemed fine, but a few days later, it kicked it."

"Ettore kills dogs," Alessandra said, balancing Francesco on her hip.

"É un serial dog killer?" I asked. The Italians seemed to understand the term *serial killer*, pronounced "say-ree-ahl keel-air."

"Sì, un serial dog killer," Alessandra agreed.

"I want that dog," I said, to my own surprise. "I want it to be my dog."

"I don't think Ettore would have a problem with that," Emanuele noted. Everyone shrugged.

I gathered up a dish of water and some leftover pasta and marched back down to the dog. Emanuele followed, smoking his cigarette. The dog remained where I had left it, long black nose balanced on the opening in the fence. I slid my hand through again, and the dog leaned in to me. It wouldn't make direct eye contact. It glanced at me sideways, bashfully. It let out a withered little sigh.

"Why didn't you tell me there was a dog down here?" I asked angrily. "Why is your family letting a dog die?"

"It's true that I am guilty, too," Emanuele said casually. "I never did do no thing for this dog."

I HAD NOT PLANNED ON a dog in my life, especially not this sort. Back in New York, I had dreamed of a rescued pit bull, those loyal urban guardians that take up almost every seat on doggy death row. But my apartment didn't allow dogs, and my lifestyle didn't welcome a dog.

Unsurprisingly, I did not immediately reflect. I did not stop to consider the pros and cons of taking on a dog in a distant land, while enmeshed in an unlikely love affair with an unsuitable fellow. In a split second, all the loneliness and aimlessness that pressed against my chest had been dissipated, and I had a single focus: my brand-new dog. My *cane nuovo*.

First thing first: None of those brutes would be allowed near my dog without my permission. My dog would know love and devotion. My dog would no longer starve. My dog would not be alone, abandoned by those who were supposed to care. My tattered dog would be reborn, would be saved, would be *molto amato*. Was this what psychiatrists referred to as transference?

"Giustina," Fabio beckoned. He looked embarrassed. "Come with me."

He led me to the food shed and pointed imploringly at a super-size bag of kibble with a cartoon of a happy Irish setter on its front.

"Vedi? Mangia!" You see? It eats!

"The dog's water is green and solid," I said.

"But the food is good food!" Fabio insisted. "Not cheap!"

"Okay, Fabio," I said. He was upset. "I believe you."

HERE IS HOW THE DISMAL tale unfolded: A year earlier, a hunting aficionado and fan of bird dogs gave Ettore a pair of English pointer puppies, two speckled eight-week-olds, which Ettore had toted around town. After a month, he grew bored with the puppies and put them in the back pen, where so many Cruciani dogs had languished over the decades. There, the two puppies grew up together, alone in the cramped space. Ettore failed to tend to them, to water or feed them, and Fabio, as always, took up their cause. But Fabio was capable of keeping creatures alive, not providing for them a quality of life. His expertise was in pigs and sheep, not dogs, and pigs and sheep could survive happily on grass, muddy water, and stale bread, huddled against one another. Pigs and sheep, as far as I could tell, did not need human affection to nourish their bestial souls.

Farm dogs in the area usually died by the age of three. As tradition dictated, they were considered livestock, more or less, or tools for hunting. They were left in outdoor cages with old water. The water and the dirty canine flesh attracted sand flies, which transmitted a virus called leishmania, common in the Mediterranean. If detected early, the disease can be treated, but these dogs were generally neglected, and when they began to show signs of the virus—weight loss, bleeding nose, inflamed eyes—the parasitic infection had taken hold. This is what happened to the emaciated dogs in the pen, or so Ettore assumed.

Instead of taking the dogs, which had been given no care since they were dumped in the pen a year earlier, to the veterinarian, Ettore decided that both dogs were on their way out. He would shoot them in the forest and end this messy ordeal. Ettore was used to shooting dogs.

I'd read memoirs of life in rural Italy, penned by American women who tended to their broken-down villas in wine country, visited the locals for a pig roast, and gazed at the cypress trees while envisioning themselves in cornflower blue smocks, skipping up and down the hills with jugs of fresh sheep's milk in their hands. I'd read stories of learning the lyrical language, of dancing into the night, of enjoying bacchanalian feasts of wine and linguine. The country is grand and diverse, and the enchanting Italy of those women exists; on my previous vacations and on my research trips with the businessman, I had enjoyed it. But Collelungo was not that Italy, and I would soon learn firsthand that there's nothing romantic about hauling any sort of fresh-squeezed animal milk.

When Collelungo's dogs fell ill, they were not carried to the pristine steel table of the veterinarian's office, not for a checkup and not for euthanasia. For the most part, Collelungo's dogs were diagnosed by citizens who had seen a dog or two die in their lifetimes. This was country wisdom, and it was hard to rail against since it had been around for centuries and I'd been around for a couple of months. Once a dog was diagnosed with an incurable illness, its owner brought it to Ettore. An owner, no matter how much or how little care he had taken of the dog, usually didn't want to shoot his own animal, so Ettore gladly loaded the forsaken pet into his rickety white Fiat Panda and took off to the dark woods to put the dog to sleep the rural way. He did the same with his own dogs.

Ettore was packing up his rifle and loading the spotted dogs into the car when Fabio wandered by. Looking at the two shaking pups, Fabio pointed to the smaller sibling.

"That one doesn't look so bad," he said. "Let it live."

Ettore dumped the dog back into its pen and sped the other out to its death. That was two weeks before I happened upon my new dog.

I slid the water and pasta into the dog's cage. It inspected the offerings curiously but was distracted by my presence and continued to glance up at me to see what I had in store for it. Emanuele and I stood together, looking at it. What was its name?

Its name was, apparently, Ettore's dog.

That would not do.

I paced around the cage, and the dog followed me from inside the fencing. The dog, despite its impoverished circumstance, had an air of refinement, a subdued ardent quality, an aspect of muffled pleading. It was also relatively neat and dignified, with a long, elegant neck and a serious expression. It looked like a worried academic, or an anemic aristocrat. Looking back at photographs, I see that the dog was not handsome then. Its fur was dry, dusted with dirt, and its bones stuck through its skin. Its eyes were swollen, and mucus oozed from their corners. In the photographs from the first days I knew the dog, its face is arranged in a permanent frown. I can see that now, but then, I managed to overlook the imperfections—a lifetime first for me, an accident—and to see only a splendid little animal. For some reason, I felt that the dog, were it human, would be a regal British man.

"Your name is . . . Archibald."

"No," Emanuele said. "Brutto."

"Henry?"

He shook his head.

"Clark."

"Sei matta."

"Marcus!" I said.

"Marquez," Emanuele said. "Un bel nome."

"Marcus," I said to the dog. It cocked its head to the side and looked confused. "That is your new name."

Emanuele, smoking, leaning against the barn, suggested that we let Marcus out of the pen. I was concerned that he would run away, but Emanuele was sure he wouldn't.

"How do you know?" I asked. "Marcus might want to escape." "Are you kidding? This dog cannot believe its luck," Emanuele reasoned. "It found an angel. It is shocked, thinking, 'Where did this angel come from? Dio, ti ringrazio di questo angelo.' It won't run away."

I opened the door to the pen. The dog was enthusiastic but controlled. He placed one paw outside, then another. I grabbed the soft nape of his neck and led him out to the open field, where the sheep grazed. Marcus was docile, following my hand without resistance. Once in the field, I studied him—a small working dog of the nervous variety, no more than twenty-five pounds, insecure and gentle. It was a leap of faith, but I let go of his neck. We looked at each other. I was, I realized, his leader by default. He needed guidance. I motioned with my arm, *go*. He straightened, raised his head, and surveyed his surroundings, the wide field stretching up to a vacant house and down into the thick woods. His black nose moved in excitement, each scent—the leaves, the olive trees, the manure, the wild grass, the far-off livestock, the rotting figs—distinct and separate from the rest. He took in the many smells with commitment, dedication, his posture noble, his tail straightening horizontally, his feet poised for maximum takeoff. Then, like a sprinter at a marathon block, he pushed away and began to run. Marcus ran with skill and speed I had never before seen in a dog. He had been waiting to run like this for his entire life.

He ran, rejoicing, in wide circles over the field, fast and graceful, his gait even. He raced in loops, looking, beyond the dust and the ribs, like a luminous and muscular thoroughbred, born to run. He crept low to the ground for a moment, stalking some imperceptible creature, a bird I couldn't see, and then broke his stride and sprinted, snout open with joy, black lips curled up to bare white teeth in a demented canine smile, long pink tongue blowing back in the wind. He mimicked the bird's swooping figure eights from his place on the ground.

"Corre bene," Emanuele said approvingly. He runs well. He'd seen many hunting dogs; this one ran with a particular talent.

I dispatched Emanuele to find a collar for Marcus somewhere in town, and I sat down in the center of the field and continued to watch the show. As I witnessed a dog pour out a year of cramped energy, of lonesomeness, I noticed, below his tail, a small, dark nub. I bent down and opened my arms, using a technique that had been successful with my childhood dogs. Marcus barreled into me, knocking me to the ground, and placed his front paws on my thighs, raising himself up to take in the landscape. I turned him around, and there it was, as I had suspected: a vagina.

"Marcus," I said, "you're a girl."

Marcus may have been female, but she looked like a proper, intellectual British fellow—well bred, distant, and focused, with her dark head held high. She continued her surveillance of the field. I placed my palm out, open, and she rested her small head in it and continued to sniff. I felt her soft muzzle, her elegant face, her crepe-paper ears. This pretty, nervous creature was mine, she was speedy, and she had a man's name.

"È femmina!" I told Emanuele when he returned, bearing the only collar he could find. An elderly couple in town owned a miniature poodle named Luigi. His companion, another miniature poodle, had passed away, but her collar remained. The couple had given Emanuele a thin pink leather collar, bejeweled with crystals. We slipped it onto Marcus's skinny neck. She stood, oblivious to her unfortunate accessory, poised to hunt, looking as awkward as a tomboy in a lavender taffeta dress, the gleaming collar wrapped around her long black neck.

MARCUS WAS WHAT I GOT, not what I imagined I wanted. I had seen myself with that confident male mutt—my protector, a little rough around the edges. Marcus was a timid purebred. Once she had been dewormed and force-fed lamb and pasta for several months, she became an objectively lovely animal, with a glossy head and velvety ears, and a highly muscled body, as balletic as a cat. Ettore, hoping to breed her ("È puro!") and sell the puppies, dug up her birth certificate. Her birth name was Brina Vipenae. Breed: pointer *inglese;* markings: *bianco nero.* She had been born in the Tuscan town of Bibbiena Stazione on June 11, 2005, which made her just over a year old when I found her, and she came from a long, serious, well-documented line of pointers. She was field bred, which meant that no relative of hers had ever been designated as a household companion. These were machines, these animals, with an instinct for birding that overtook everything. No matter what Marcus was involved in, including gnawing on a large ham bone, if she saw a bird, her body straightened into a hard arrow. She'd freeze, slowly raising her right front paw, tilting her taut body forward, a straight line. The idea was that the pointer pointed out the game, and then either it or a flushing dog rushed the bird and sent it flying into the air, only to be shot down, gently retrieved, and cooked. I'd grown up with a large, friendly pound dog and a hypoallergenic terrier that looked like a baby lamb—normal dogs, really, who liked a little jog, a little sniff, a nice piece of bread or roast beef, a short wrestle with another canine, and a seat by the fire.

Marcus was not of that ilk. She was like a world-class professional athlete: born to be the best, her body formed for exactly one reason. She was the Olympic cyclist, racing up the mountain, her brain of that moment, her chiseled body rising to the summit; other dogs were the rest of us, laid out on the couch with a microwaved enchilada and a Corona. They were all technically members of the same species, but Marcus was imbued with something extraordinary.

When there was a bird in the vicinity, Marcus had a purpose, a job, a role in the galaxy. She wasn't wild or goofy, obsessed with treats or sloppy. Rather, she was disciplined and serious, with a limited sense of humor. Other dogs wanted to play with her, but Marcus had no use for them. Some initially attempted to roughhouse and soon slunk away, dejected, as she ignored them entirely and concentrated on more pressing matters: the never-ending hunt. Her most innate pleasure was in accomplishment, not socializing. She was on a mission, wherever she went, and that mission was simple and defined: She was to find and stalk all things bird. If she saw a distracted bluebird pecking at the earth, she lowered her unyielding body to the ground and began to approach it in the terrifying manner in which a Saharan lion creeps toward a gazelle: with perfect concentration and complete, overwhelming rapaciousness, one paw after another, a smooth, gliding motion, her chest and belly inches from the earth, her muzzle perfectly parallel to the ground. Her focus was so complete that she could withstand anything when she entered this state: I witnessed 130-pound dogs barking in her ear, and terriers humping her with glee; she tuned them out entirely as she crept toward her prey. Inevitably, the bird launched at the last moment, and Marcus broke from her stance and ran.

Running was her other favorite activity. She sprinted at thirty-five miles per hour for as long as she possibly could. When she was not single-mindedly chasing after a bird or a flock of birds, or circling the neighbor's chicken coop like a hired hit man, her main passion was to accompany those on horseback for hours—only an Arabian could give her a worthy challenge. Pointers were capable of high speeds and possessed of remarkable endurance. It was not only that Marcus was faster than any dog I'd ever seen; it was that she wished to run ceaselessly at that speed for hours. If any horse passed the house, she went with it. Immediately after she had discovered the joy of the horse chase, she could identify the sound of approaching hooves and would abandon whatever patch of grass or haystack upon which she was resting and dash out to greet her reluctant playmate.

At first, I kept her in the pen. She was not allowed in the house, so as soon as I woke, I drove to the bar, where Cinzia, the owner, gave me my *International Herald Tribune,* my strong cappuccino, and my flaky apple pastry, warmed up and served on a napkin on which it left a greasy mark in the shape of a triangle. When I'd finished my breakfast, standing at the bar as townspeople ran in and out—the women stopping longer for cappuccinos and the men downing sugary, bitter espressos in half a minute—I headed for Marcus, scurrying down to her pen as though she were my long-lost lover. Without fail, there she stood, tense and ready, her head cocked as she heard footsteps, never sure whose they were, but hoping with all her heart that they were mine. Whenever she saw me, her face registered a brief look of utter shock, as though she'd hoped I would round the corner, but had never really thought it might be so.

When she knew she would be released from her little prison, she broke into a dance of joy. Each morning was just as exciting as the last, and she jumped upon me exuberantly, stretching out her long, gangly puppy legs. Then she bolted out onto the path, turned to check that I was bringing up the rear, and headed out to the meadow, where she ran up to the neighbor's olive grove, down into the forest, and around the perimeter of the property, always returning to me. I sat on the ground by a lone olive tree if the grass was not too wet, and tried to read the paper, despite the fact that her paws landed on the news every few minutes. Marcus liked to check in. She liked to rest her front paws on my thighs and take in the air, or she liked to lean in to me, resting her head on my shoulder. If I pressed her close, she let out a heavy, satisfied sigh.

Over the next few weeks, Emanuele and Ettore, in a display of indulgence, helped me to expand her cage. We picked out yards of green fencing at the hardware store and drove it back to Collelungo in the miniature car. The fencing, at ten feet high, was longer than the car, so I sat in the open back in the suddenly frigid early winter air, grabbing the roll of wire as Emanuele navigated the curved roads.

"You are very country, my love," he yelled out happily. On the radio, the international pop-rock star Zucchero sang of a scattered, desperate, delicate heart. *Questo cuore disperato è delicato.* My fingers went numb from the cold.

Ettore and Emanuele spent five hours putting up the fence to make a nice cage for Marcus, a dog they didn't care about. But I did care, and I did believe in her, so they worked. It was a classic example of the Collelungese principle of selflessness, which almost couldn't be considered a principle in that the citizens didn't even seem to notice that they were doing someone a favor. It was as if, when it came to helping others, people were indistinguishable as individuals. When Ettore helped Emanuele and me build Marcus's new pen, he seemed unaware that he was spending his Friday evening doing hard labor for another person. Instead, he approached the work as though it were for his own benefit. Because Emanuele and I were a couple, I was the equivalent of Emanuele, who in turn was a part of Ettore. So if I needed something, Ettore would do it without question or complaint or any expectation of thanks.

Marta, who operated as an extension of Ettore (and vice versa), came along, too, and devoted three hours to lugging all the old, useless objects on the property—moldy wooden planks, cracked plastic buckets, paintbrushes, a ripped mattress, empty bags of feed—to a pile. Then, we topped off the junk mountain with Marcus's old wooden box, soaked it with lighter fluid, and lit a bonfire, which was for me symbolic (Marcus's old life of sadness and detachment would be destroyed) but was for Ettore and Emanuele just a lot of fun. Then Serenella called us in for dinner. The garbage, engulfed in flames, burned on the dewy hillside into the early morning.

As a replacement, I found an unfinished doghouse that Emanuele had made for another dog years earlier. It was also a wooden box, but this one had a slanted metal roof, an insulated side, and feet to keep it off the dirt. I painted it cream and blue, and fixed up a sign that said "Marcus's Casa," with two black paw prints flanking the text. Ettore remarked that I was ridiculous. Serenella, witnessing the care I lavished on an animal, voiced her disapproval.

"Sei matta per quell'cane," she said, shaking her head. But she saved her leftovers for Marcus and handed me a plate of pasta, which Marcus would eat daintily later, always glancing to each side to make sure that she was safe. It was true: I was crazy for the dog. I sewed a pillow for Marcus's bed and stuffed it inside the *casa*.

Marcus chewed up the pillow, leaving her plot of earth covered in puffs of synthetic filling, but otherwise accepted her change in fortune with patience and goodwill. For some time, however, she was skeptical of the new house, and slept on the roof.

⌒⌒

AT THE BEGINNING OF MY relationship with the dog, I drove to *il Dottor* Andrea Massarelli, a slight young blond man six towns over, who operated a two-room veterinary practice in a space off a warehouse. He inspected Marcus, who trembled upon the steel table but did not resist, her skinny haunches causing reverberations throughout the room, her tail curved up sharply between her legs. He gently pushed on her eyes, round with fear, stared into her floppy black ears with a flashlight, felt her empty belly, and declared her fundamentally healthy but for the eye infection, the ear infection, and the raging case of worms.

"Good thing they didn't shoot you in the brush," I muttered to her as we made our way back to Collelungo. Marcus lay tightly curled on the passenger side floor, with her entire head shoved beneath the seat. She didn't think road trips were fun.

Three times a day, I ventured down to her cage, where I pried

open her eyes, pressing against the black upper lashes to smear oint-
ment around them, and flipped over her ears to squirt medicine into
them, staring into the intricate interior, all crevices and valleys that
led inside, creating that exquisitely effective organ that could sense a
whistle miles away. For all this, Marcus stood stock still, enduring
what was incomprehensible to her. I hid the pill in a piece of prosciutto and gave it to her; she took it lightly, her mouth so soft—they
were bred that way, so they didn't damage the hunter's kill—that it
took her several tries to bite down adequately. I purchased a shiny red
collar to wrap around her neck. I had a tag engraved for her in Todi:
Marcus, Collelungo, my Italian cell phone number. This dog belonged
to someone, the collar advertised; this dog was not up for grabs.

Even apart from her acute hunting obsessions, Marcus was not
your average dog, galumphing, licking, full of good cheer. She was
frankly terrified of human beings—probably because her earliest
owner considered cats game and had blasted away her starving sister
in the woods. When she was free, running, hunting, or snoozing in
the garden, she was relaxed and happy. But at the bar, when we sat
outside at night with the locals, she clung to my lap, front paws heavy
like iron across my thighs, chest pressed into me, eyes wary. I walked
down the street with her, and she pulled the leash taut, trying to get
away from any person in the vicinity. She walked in a crouch, ready
to bolt at any second, and kept her tail tucked beneath her in public.
Once, I tied her to a bench outside the grocery shop and ran in for
some bread. An old man rushed behind, motioning to me.

"Il cane!" he bellowed. "Il cane!" The dog, you American luna-
tic! The dog! The dog!

Outside, Marcus had dragged the metal bench down the road by
her neck. She stood several yards from the store, attached to the object,
her entire body convulsing. She stared at me in shock and horror; how
could I have put her in such a terrible predicament? I ran through the
square with my loaf of bread, toward my traumatized ward.

"I'm so sorry," I said as I unclipped her leash. She stood to the side, head cocked, as I dragged the bench back to its rightful spot outside the grocer's door. The old men who spent their days watching the cars go by enjoyed the show. I considered bowing, so entranced were they by the spectacle.

Later, I laid her on the ground and gave her a makeshift canine massage, pulling out her back legs, rubbing her ears. She melted, letting out soft moans, and laid her head on my lap. I had been so insensitive. I had so dumbly put her in such a terrifying situation, tied up and vulnerable next to a group of loud old guys. I scratched beneath her chin, where a few stray whiskers grew. Serenella watched from the window, shaking her head.

The villagers thought I was out of my mind. *That dog, that girl and that dog.* Dogs, in their opinions, were to be chained up or caged. They were creatures, like sheep and cows, that served a purpose for human beings: hunting partner, guard, truffle finder. They were not cuddly friends or substitutes for children; you were not to pour your savings into their comfort or purchase trinkets for them. They were beasts. *Delle bestie.*

I felt people's skepticism, but I was beyond concern. There was the ritual of my devotion, the hillside walk, the little creature behind the door, wild with excitement at the prospect of her release. We were immediately bound by our loneliness and our need—she, a neglected animal who depended on me for sustenance, and I, an isolated expat with no one else upon whom to satisfactorily project my affections. More than that, I think what bound us was something mysterious and less scientific.

"She's a good dog," Fabio said one day as we stood on the drive. *Un cane buono.* "She is a true innocent."

"The barbarian could hurt a baby," Serenella said. "You should chain her."

I shook my head—unthinkable. Serenella didn't trust Marcus.

Francesco, now toddling with the help of an adult holding his hands, hoped to embrace Marcus and ran after her screaming, "Macks! Macks!" Serenella held him back, convinced that my shrinking animal would turn at any moment and eat her grandchild.

"But you don't even put him in a car seat," I argued. Whenever people drove short distances with babies, they balanced the babies freely on their laps and steered; yet, upon seeing Marcus approach timidly to sniff them, they yelled, "Via!" Away! Collelungo was not the place to have a dog. In fact, Italy, like most countries, had some regional issues with humane treatment of animals; down in some southern provinces, the local animal rescues had begun a campaign to convince citizens to stop abandoning their dogs to the street when the people went on vacation, as it had become custom to let the pet fend for itself while the owner was out of town.

"Vai pazza per quell'cane," everyone said. You've gone nuts for that dog. Shouldn't I be making friends with the local girls? Learning how to cook or drive a stick shift? Really, shouldn't I be devoting myself to anything else? Anything at all?

But Fabio shrugged and lit another cigar.

"Si ama chi si ama," he said. One loves whom one loves.

⌒〜〇

MARCUS CEMENTED MY REPUTATION AS a weirdo. What's more unusual than a young American woman landing in a two-hundred-person Umbrian farming village? Only a young American woman prancing around the village with the whacked-out little hunting dog she found around back.

They fixed me in their collective gaze. They stared with the entitlement of a paying audience—their brows furrowed, following every movement. "Ma chi è quella?" they murmured. "Chi è?" But who is that? "E il cane?" And now, what's with the dog?

I vecchi, the old guys, as they were called, gathered outside the grocery store, Spesso Buia, to smoke and look across the street at the *centro storico*. When I passed by, they followed me with their eyes but kept quiet. It was a relatively diverse group: Among the rotation of forty seniors, there was an energetic marathon runner with dark curls and a small mustache tucked neatly beneath his long nose; a debonair grandfather with a bright white mass of hair and an elegant patterned shirt; a few fellows of the bald, squat, agrarian variety; and one madman who dressed in a succession of neon sweat suits, his coarse gray hair standing on end. Once, wearing a purple velour number, he tried to enter my car and had to be dragged away by the other *vecchi*.

"Scusa, signorina! Scusa," they cried, grappling with the cheery madman, as I maintained a tight smile from the driver's seat.

The women gathered in little grottos, wearing their slacks and heavy pumps or coordinated jogging suits. They sat in compact groups, four or five on a small bench, with others on nearby plastic lawn chairs or perched on the sidewalk. They didn't have anything in their hands—no mugs of coffee or knitting needles. Instead, they focused on gossip. Like *kitsch* and *stress, gossip* was a word that the Italians had made their own. *C'è sempre gossip.* They were gossip machines, the women, and they knew every single detail about every single person in town: who had been institutionalized for a nervous disorder, whose wife was schtupping the plumber, who had gained weight, who was plunging further into debt. That guy eyeing me at the bar? He repeatedly stole a teenage girl's underwear from a clothesline; he'd never been right in the head. That woman peering over the hill? She had a nervous disorder, probably due to her husband's addiction to prostitutes. But there was little judgment inherent in Collelungo's gossip; the women neither pitied nor vilified their subjects, but merely noted, sometimes with a touch of scorn or delight, their relative troubles. They were mainly observers, not empathizers. And they loved to blabber.

Later, of course, I'd come to realize that blabbering and staring was pretty much a divine right in a small town. After nine months, I found myself sitting outside the bar, and when a new car passed or a stranger entered, I strained my neck and looked them up and down—no shame, no hidden glances, a straight-up stare—and turned to the barista and said, "Who *is* that?"

One day early on, as I stumbled toward my apartment, my arms full of books, Marcus scampering ahead, two old ladies passed behind me, arms hooked together, one leaning on a cane.

"Ma chi è?" asked one loudly, repeating the popular refrain.

"L'americana," the other said. "Non capisce niente." The American; she doesn't understand a thing.

I whipped around. "I'm learning!" I said in shaky Italian.

The women gasped, whispered apologies, and scurried away.

❧

I WAS LEARNING BECAUSE I had no choice in the matter. The embarrassment I felt mangling words was overtaken by necessity. In Collelungo, nobody spoke English. The younger generation may have studied it in school, but that meant they could say only the basics: "Hello." "How are you?" "My name is Chiara." From what they had seen on television, they had also learned *hot dog* (*otdock*) and *hamburger* ('*am bourgur*).

"That's what you eat in America, right?" Emanuele's cousin Silvia asked. "Otdocks? 'Am bourgurs?"

"Scusa?"

"You know, American food: otdocks and 'am bourgurs!"

At the beginning, I communicated through Emanuele, who could understand enough of my slow English, accompanied by elaborate hand motions, to translate. But unless I learned the Italian necessary to talk to everyone else, I suspected that I would go mad. I did not have money for proper language lessons, so I hired a local girl who worked as a translator to teach me the basics in five sessions.

Having studied English in Malta, she could not actually speak the language fluently, but she had textbooks that taught verb structure. Once I'd memorized the most fundamental words and phrases, I forced myself to talk to people, and this is how I really learned Italian: from the locals.

What I did not realize was that the locals spoke in dialect. It was the only Italian I had ever spoken or really listened to, so as far as I knew, it was normal. Unbeknownst to me, it was the linguistic equivalent of learning English from the citizens of Appalachia. Before I knew it, I was obliviously speaking in heavily accented slang. Whenever I left Collelungo, Romans and Florentines looked at me, startled. If the situations had been reversed, an Italian would walk into a sleek Manhattan wine bar and say, straight-faced, with a strong Italian lilt, "Howdy, how y'all doin'?"

Worse, I picked up impolite verbal tics because I spent the majority of my time talking to older, uneducated citizens who didn't care for proper grammar or sophistication. For example, for some time I unknowingly ended all my Italian sentences with a short, nasal "eh."

"Hey you, come on over here, eh?"

"Pass me the bread, eh?"

"Lemme sit down, eh?"

"You cannot continue to say 'eh,'" Emanuele cautioned. "You sound like my grandfather, but more rude."

Or I referred to people as "this one" or "that one"—*questo, quello.*

From a native, it sounded casual. From me, it sounded bizarre, misguided. I had acquired the colloquialisms, but did not know where to put them. Of course, shielded by my ignorance, I ambled around, proudly talking like a berserk, accented sailor.

7

THE HIDDEN HARMONY IS BETTER
THAN THE OBVIOUS ONE.

—HERACLITUS

STILL, MY PRESENCE WAS REMARKABLE mostly because nothing particularly new ever happened in Collelungo, and the citizens liked it that way. Though they accepted me with grace, they remained disconcerted by my gypsy existence. It didn't sit right with them; how did my mama feel, some of the women wondered, with her *figlia* so far from home? When I explained that I would see her at least twice that year, they became upset. Twice? *Madonna mia,* a mother must see her child daily to survive.

"Chi lascia la strada vecchia per la nuova sa quel che lascia, ma non sa quel che trova" was a popular Italian saying. He who leaves the old street for the new one knows what he left but not what he'll find.

Italians in general did not admire innovation or novelty. Nor did they crave adventure. Serenella and Fabio had never flown in an airplane and had left the country only once, to visit a relative who had married a German and moved to a suburb of Munich, where he sold Etruscan-style ceramics for German homes.

"We drank the coffee there and almost died," Serenella told me, her face twisted in horror. "Fa schifo. Fa schifo!" It's disgusting!

Didn't they hope to learn of new cultures, to eat new food?

"Why would you want anything but Italian food—ever?" Ettore asked.

"Have you *tried* anything but Italian food?"

"Well, I don't see any reason."

The only international cuisine available for miles was at a small Chinese restaurant in Umbria's capital, Perugia. The restaurant existed only as a way for Umbrians to prove that other food was just rotten. Each person in Collelungo took a once-in-a-lifetime journey to the establishment, ate something really gross, and emerged with an air of satisfaction: Once again, we know that Italy rules.

Sometimes I grew frustrated—didn't they know what they were missing? Then again, didn't I know what I was missing? That Italian reverence for antiquity, for tradition, was almost a unique emotion, one without a name, and I could never experience it fully.

ONE WEEKDAY I TOOK A break from working on the businessman's book. I had been sitting in our chilly apartment for weeks on end, leaving only for meals and to visit Marcus. I drove with no particular destination in mind, ending up in the nearby town of Civitella del Lago, which sits between Orvieto and Todi. The tiny city, a fully contained stone town perched on the peak of a dense green mountain directly above the flat blue Lake Corbara, is permanently enveloped in a mist rising up from the water. Houses and medieval arches line the town borders, which are simply low brick walls upon which those not suffering vertigo can sit, breathing in the humid air and looking out at the steep, dusky drop down to the lake. The freshly swept streets are made of ancient, graying yellow brick.

On the day I visited, I wandered the streets in a daze, undone by the peculiarity of the town—this antique fortress in which, because of its contained structure, nothing new had ever been built. I passed by a squat, hirsute man in a white tank top, carrying a basket of tomatoes.

"Those are beautiful tomatoes," I said.

"You like them?" he asked. "Come with me!"

Though my inclinations as a New Yorker were to flee from a strange hairy man, I followed him down the path to a house.

"O, Ma!" he hollered up at the house. I heard some shuffling, and a tiny, disheveled old woman in a patterned housecoat and round spectacles opened the door.

"O, what you want?" she asked.

"The *signorina* likes our vegetables, Ma," the man said. "Come down!"

Ma, still in slippers, made her way down the staircase and circled around beneath it. She took a key from her pocket and opened the *cantina,* a storage room typically at street level.

"Come, come," the man motioned, as he followed Ma into the damp, windowless basement. I took a step in, hovering by the door in case this seemingly innocent duo had a murderous plan. But instead of binding and gagging me, the man ran over to a series of buckets and began to fill a plastic bag.

"These tomatoes, I grow them on my family's land on the edge of the mountain," he said. "And these potatoes we dig up from there. The eggs are from our chickens, and they are the best eggs you will ever have. The yolks are red. And you can't boil them—they're too fresh."

He filled the plastic sack with oblong tomatoes, yellow and green zucchini, petite black eggplants, and potatoes. In another sack, he placed six brown eggs.

"Where are you from?" he asked.

His mother grinned upon hearing that I was from New York.

"Come back here," he yelled, and I surrendered myself to fate—which was seeming less likely to lead me to death and more likely to lead me to produce—following deeper into the *cantina,* where bicycles lined the walls and a motorcycle sat beneath a dusty tarp. In the coolest, darkest area, he kept two cisterns. He pulled out a plastic cup and poured pale yellow wine into it.

"Drink it," he commanded, hands on hips. "It is some of the finest wine you will ever taste in your life!" Ma, meanwhile, stood to the side, awaiting my confirmation of this fact.

The wine was clean, strange, very pure, and dry. "È magnifico, questo vino," I said. What grapes had he used?

"Our grapes, indigenous to Civitella," he said. "My family has grown them for centuries." Then he filled a glass bottle and handed it to me.

"You cannot give me all this!" I protested, as I was pushed out onto the sidewalk.

"I must," he exclaimed. "This way, you will taste my vegetables and my wine, and you will go back to New York City and tell all the people, 'The best in the world comes from Civitella del Lago!'"

I continued to walk, ever more dazed and now carrying ten pounds of vegetables and a bottle of wine, down the street, passing a marmalade cat, and again reaching the wall that separated the town from the near-vertical slope leading to the lake. I stopped to admire a narrow, freestanding three-story stone house, outside of which sat an impressive collection of purple, magenta, and white geraniums in burnt, orange pots. A dream catcher, dripping with pearly feathers, hung over the door, and a stained glass charm dangled inside the closest window. A round woman with long, dark curls emerged from the house carrying a watering can.

"Your house is lovely," I said.

"Oh, thank you," she said. "Is this your first time in Civitella?"

It was my first time walking the streets, though I had once

before passed through, and I told her that I loved the city, and that a man had just given me tomatoes, and that I could understand why someone would never move away.

"I worked in Rome for eight years," she said as she began to pour water over the geraniums. "And every single day I cried. I cried, 'I miss my Civitella, I want my Civitella!'"

$$\sim$$

I HAD ONCE LIVED WITH a Pakistani girl in Manhattan, and within a month, her mother and father had taken a generous vacation from their lives in Lahore and had settled into our two-bedroom in Murray Hill. Her mother cooked spicy halal chicken while her father lounged on our living room futon and watched the Home Shopping Network with a blackhead-removing strip stuck to his nose. It had been an entirely unpleasant experience for me, as a solitary only child, to sign up for one roommate and get three, but I understood that the bonds between this group were different from those that I knew.

"We don't have nursing homes in Pakistan," my roommate once informed me.

They did not have nursing homes in Italy, either, as far as I could tell. Certainly nobody in the history of Collelungo had been surrendered to such doom. While my grandmother Mildred gazed out at treetops from the window of her carpeted room at a dreary luxury facility (tagline: *Senior Living. Distinctive Lifestyles.*) in the corporate center of Stamford, Connecticut, Emanuele's grandparents were surrounded by dozens of relatives. When Nonna Ferrina came down with the flu, Serenella trudged up to her house twice a day to prepare food for her mother and Nonno Marcello, who was a useless caretaker. Her sister-in-law Giovanna stopped in with supplies whenever Serenella was at work. Giovanna's daughter Emanuela kept Ferrina company when she was bored, breaking up the long stretches during which she was bedridden and could not partake in her daily gabfest with the other ladies out on the corner. Various friends limped by, took coffee, smoked a cigarette by the bedside, dispensed gossip in their raspy voices, compared aches and pains.

Fabio's parents, Maria and Renato, had always lived up the hill from Fabio and Serenella's house. Renato, with his brilliant silver hair and thick mustache, had the constitution of a manual laborer, and even though he was legally blind, he liked to hoe a small vegetable garden on the land between his property and Fabio's property.

Renato's wife, Maria, who had been a housewife, was afflicted with dementia, and when she needed to be cared for, Fabio brought his parents to live with him. She was a tiny, delicate woman who weighed ninety-five pounds. Her face was round and freckled, her ashen hair curled and short. Her limbs did not seem capable of bending sufficiently, and she needed help to shuffle from room to room. Her eyes reflected little emotion, and her lips were permanently parted, as though she was always on the verge of speech. She appeared imprisoned in a thick mental fog but was not unaware of her state. Instead, she was anxious, vaguely cognizant of the fact that her mind—that in fact, her self—was fading.

Once, Emanuele and I were communicating in pidgin English when we saw the mute Maria staring at us.

"Maybe she knows English and she's fooling us all!" I exclaimed, and we began to laugh, but then I turned and saw that Maria's once-blank expression had folded into one of penetrating despair.

For the last three months of Maria's life, she was never alone. She slept fitfully in the downstairs bedroom, across the hall from Fabio and Serenella's room. During the night, she often called out and wanted to walk the halls in her heavy flannel nightgown. Fabio guided his mother as she navigated the floor, and then put her back into bed, as his elderly father sat up nearby, his eyes glassy. In the morning, Serenella bathed and dressed Maria, combed her hair, applied lotion to her face. Throughout the day, someone from the family checked in on Maria, and every week, they brought Maria to their salon and washed and curled her hair. Her clothes were pressed; her shoes were shined.

When they were young, Emanuele had told me, Maria had lived five miles away from Collelungo's center, and Renato had been too poor to own a horse. He had walked to visit her every day. Now, for months on end, without a break, Renato stayed next to Maria.

"Oh, those two used to fight constantly," Serenella once said. "Yelling, screaming, and then 'I'm sorry,' 'No, I'm sorry.' Then the next day, they would be at it again."

Now, at almost any hour, you could walk into the Crucianis' house to find Renato and Maria seated across from the door on a bright orange love seat. They each claimed a cushion, Maria propped up with pillows and Renato sinking into the couch, his woolen cap balanced on his lap. He refused to leave her—neither to attend church nor to till the dirt of his vegetable plot. He sat in silence, staring vaguely at the television that was too far away for him to see and waiting for Maria to utter a single word or an absent demand. If she wanted to take a walk around the house, he lifted her up on his shaky arm and supported her as they made the rounds, from the kitchen to the hallway and back. If she wanted to take another walk immediately upon sitting down, he steadied himself again, and again offered his arm. For the months that they lived in Casa Cruciani, I never once saw Maria and Renato apart, not even for five minutes.

When Maria died, Renato refused to see her body at the hospital viewing room, nor did he attend her funeral. I did: First I saw her laid out on a metal table under the fluorescent lights and later in a small coffin, her face waxen, her eyes shut, wearing a deep purple dress that Serenella had chosen for her. Her smooth, round, liver-spotted hands clutched a red rosary, the golden cross reflecting the light. Fabio stood next to her, his face wet; Serenella was calm, composed. At the funeral, where dozens lined the pews, the African priest praised Maria and her passage to heaven, his French accent so thick that even the Italians had trouble understanding him. Fabio and his brother and sister sat in the front pew. When we stood, I saw Serenella briefly clutch her husband's hand.

After the funeral, Renato sat in his son Gianni's kitchen in a fake leather chair. He held his cap again in his hand, staring a faraway stare. I sat nearby, on the ledge in front of the fireplace. Some older friends drank coffee and water and ate almond cookies that Gianni's wife, Tiziana, had made. Renato refused any offerings, slumped forward, and began to weep, as though Maria's death was a horrible surprise. She had been dying and suffering for so long, I reasoned, that her death would come, at least in part, as some relief, but I was mistaken. Everyone looked at him with blasé acceptance. Awkwardly, I placed my hand on his back. He moved away slightly, buried his head in his weatherworn hands, and cried out, "Non è giusto!" It isn't fair.

Later that year, when Renato went into the hospital for a week to recover from a bout of pneumonia, I accompanied Emanuele to see him during visiting hours. He lay in a common ward, separated by a paper-white curtain from six other elderly men, all laid out flat or propped up on their single beds in their thin gowns.

"Ciao, Renato," I said, nestled among seven of his grandchildren, one of his daughters-in-law, and both of his sons, all of us pressed together in the cramped space.

"Oh! Is that Giustina?" he exclaimed, able to make out only the contours of my face. "Giustina, how lovely that you came."

In Italy, it seemed, if you weren't family, you were at the very least, innately, from birth, a friend.

MOGLI E BUOI DEI PAESI TUOI.
—ITALIAN PROVERB: GET YOUR WIVES AND OXEN
FROM YOUR OWN VILLAGE.

BUT, AS THE ITALIANS OFTEN said: There's always another side to the coin. Family and friends were thick, but everyone had their roles to play. Even me, apparently.

Fa' la brava moglie. Be a good wife. Be a good, proud wife, who cooks and cleans and can darn a sock, who chats with her friends, who feeds the children, then the nieces and nephews, then the grandchildren, and even the great-grandchildren, who watches TV, who makes the house nice—but not too nice, not show-off nice, just nice enough, and so spotless that you can eat a pork dinner directly off the floor. Don't want more. Don't hope to leave one day or to find a wealthy husband, or to make a pile of cash on your own. *Fa' la brava moglie* and like it. Like it like the men soldering iron like it. Like it like the men chopping wood like it. Like it like the factory workers like it. It's your job, so like it.

Most women took on the role proudly, without question, and performed instinctively—the washing, ironing, polishing, cooking, the limitless caretaking. The most I'd done in terms of taking care of someone was hailing a cab for an inebriated friend, but I wasn't there to rage against their cultural systems; perhaps being *la brava moglie* was a source of satisfaction of which I simply couldn't conceive—yet. The phrase "When in Rome, do as the Romans do" had new meaning. I would try to learn a new trade out in those pretty hills, surrounded by so many ladies stirring broth and patching pants.

I needed a role model, because I didn't know where to start, and Emanuele certainly couldn't help. So I would search for my teacher.

I did not have to search far. She sat at the heavy kitchen table at least twice a week. She didn't know it, but Marta, Ettore's Marta, would be my mentor. In Umbria, one did not have to literally be a wife to play the wife. Serious boyfriends and girlfriends were referred to widely as fiancés and fiancées, and any pair that lived together was essentially considered a husband and wife. With that in mind, I courted Marta to be my friend. It was not an easy courtship.

I first saw Marta sitting on a small bench in town. She and Ettore had broken up a few months before I arrived, so Emanuele pointed her out to me from afar, a young woman in tight blue jeans and white running sneakers, her wild black curls pushed back into a messy bun, not a speck of makeup. She had an angular jaw and high cheekbones, brown eyes framed by thick black brows. Her body was lithe, her shoulders broad, her waist small. She sat still, her face impassive.

"Ettore's ex," Emanuele said. "I think she is a little dull." On the contrary, I would learn.

Marta, a beautician in the nearby town of Orvieto, kept a small photograph of Ettore tucked into her mirror at her manicure station; they had been together for almost ten years, since they were teenagers. Eventually, a client pointed to the picture.

"I went out with that man," the client observed.

Highly doubtful; that man was taken. Marta wanted to know when.

"A few weeks ago," the client said, turning slowly to see the color drain from Marta's face. "*O, madonna mia*, is he your boyfriend?"

Until then, Marta had trusted Ettore naively, implicitly, the way a fifteen-year-old cherishes her first, and only, love. She was twenty-five and had never been with another man, not even for a gelato.

"If he had asked me to put my hand into a fire, I would have done it without question," she later told me.

She cut him off. Ettore, hanging on to his pride by a thin thread, refused to grovel in public, and they spent a year passing each other with only the coldest of mutual acknowledgments.

For the first month of my time in Italy, I never saw Marta and Ettore together. Emanuele was convinced that his brother would have to find another woman. Instead, behind the scenes, Ettore was quietly working to convince Marta to give their relationship a final shot. In public, he ignored her; in private, he promised her that he would change: no more discos on his own, no more drugs, no more girls. Finally, she relented. I watched as they descended Via Todi bareback on his white Arabian mare, slowly making their way to the house, her arms wrapped around his waist.

"I think he looked everywhere and he found that for him, only Marta," Emanuele said.

So when Marta reentered the Cruciani family, she did so with trepidation. She had spent half of her life in and out of that house and had little patience for the wild disorganization that was the Cruciani way of life.

"It's not Italy in that house," a woodworker, who happened to be the town fascist, told me. "It's worse! It's Albania, for God's sake!"

In Marta's mind, I was part and parcel of that disorganization; she had friends, sisters, a mother, a job—what did she need me for? The first time I saw her up close, I had walked out of the house and happened upon rangy Ettore dressed in military-style hunting gear.

He stood, polishing his rifle and smoking a cigarette, while Marta, also in military-style hunting gear, sat nonchalantly on a chaise longue, carving a small stick with a pocketknife. She looked at me hard and gave me a chin jut, and then returned to the stick.

"Marta is an aesthetician," Emanuele said, by way of introduction.

"Really! I *love* aestheticians," I blurted out. Marta refused to grace me with even the weakest of smiles.

The next time I saw her, she was carrying a bucket of water up from the horse barn, dressed in blue jeans and a sweat-soaked tank top, Ettore's heavy black cop boots—a hand-me-down from a *carabiniere*—laced tight all the way up her legs. Her dark skin shone, her long curls were pressed into braids, the rebellious strands slowly pushing their way out from the plaits.

"È molto country," Emanuele said, laughing. He found it entertaining to watch me and Marta interact, passing each other on the dirt path, past the feed room. She was the strong indigenous plant, with deep roots in this land, and I was some ethereal exotic flower wilting in the unfamiliar climate. I had tried to wear my mauve ballet flats down to the horse barn that day, but had sunk into the mud. I could feel each pebble beneath the thin soles, and I put them in the back of my closet when I got home. It would be sneakers from now on.

Marta was *molto* country, indeed. She joined the group for a dinner of sparrow that Ettore had shot in the fields. Serenella had roasted the tiny game over the fire, and I sat nervously in front of my dish. As always, the family enjoyed watching me work up my courage. They leaned in as I chewed.

"Pretty good," I ventured. I was cool; couldn't throw me for a loop with a common bird.

"You want to try some brain?" Ettore asked. "It's delicious." He crushed the skull and pulled out the mushy roasted gray matter.

"Do you really eat it?"

"We don't," said Serenella, "but Marta does. Her whole family does."

Marta took the brain from Ettore and popped it in her mouth. Then she plucked the brain from her own sparrow and ate that, too. "It's the best part," she said, sucking on a leg bone and peering at my plate. "Are you going to eat yours?"

Despite a penchant for medulla oblongata and a deep-seated refusal to smile more than humanly necessary, Marta wasn't particularly harsh. I learned this during our weekly beautification sessions, which I requested meekly upon learning of her practice. Marta agreed, and I began my visits to her makeshift salon up the road.

I drove the heaving Twingo to the compound in which she had grown up, an eyesore that surged up from the dry greenery like a fortress, made of stone and stucco and heavy shutters, protecting its inhabitants from the outer world. The Nini family lived there, on the top floor, which was spotless and comfortable, with large windows that overlooked the valley. The Nini women had similar masses of black hair, olive skin, and black eyes. Onello Nini was the lone male of the clan. Brawny and serious, he seemed constantly to be hauling wood and watering his animals. The Ninis were savvy, pragmatic, and dedicated to hard work and making money, which is where Marta had acquired her nose for business. Her father had saved for decades in order to build a mansion in the Collelungo countryside. The Ninis spent years laying stone for an old-style estate, painting its rooms yellow and red, tiling the floors, installing wooden ceiling beams and a state-of-the-art stainless steel kitchen. They then marketed Villa Diana on their Web site, which included hospitality quotes by Brillat-Savarin and impressive English prose: *Villa Diana has been recently built on a charming unspoilt rural area. Our countryside still has a timeless feel to it, the smells and the aromas of the fields and woods being untainted by modern living.* The Ninis welcomed the Americans and British and

Germans with wide, innocent smiles and the sausages they'd made in
their simple flat across the way. They were there to rake in the dollars
and the euros.

Marta had taken this acumen and transformed her late grandmother's house into a makeshift salon. "Sono in nero," she told me.
In the black, illegal. My first time at the speakeasy salon, I knocked
on the old oak door and heard Marta cry, "Avanti!" I stepped into
the dark, cool house and plugged my nose: The unventilated apartment, its ancient furniture covered with sheets, smelled of must and
mildew. Marta stood in a single, lit room off the main hallway, with
sponge-painted pink walls, a massage table, and a series of tools and
medical lights. I momentarily panicked, wondering if it was wise to
let her mangle my skin, and then gave in: What choice did I have in
Collelungo? This was no sterile Manhattan dermatologist's office,
nor was it a gleaming nail salon run by chatty young immigrants
who brandished their pumice stones with aggression, just waiting to
scrub your feet raw. There were no wealthy ladies with immobile
foreheads bumping elbows with me in the waiting room, or Upper
East Side daughters receiving their bimonthly seaweed wraps. Still,
I craved some sort of beautification, and Marta was the only game in
town. Plus, she gave me a discount.

As I lay on the table every week—for a pedicure, a feeble massage, or microdermabrasion treatments that Marta performed with a
small portable machine that she had picked up from a DermaNew
representative—I entered that universal salon, where all women from
all cultures all over the world go to be touched and primped, for
their men or because their men neglect them, or because they derive
pleasure from the intimate feminine rituals of hair removal, skin
softening, nail filing. Marta reminded me of the many women in my
life who had hovered over me, the nurses and manicurists and wax-
ers and hairdressers who had placed their hands on my face or my
head or the most sensitive region of my inner thigh and who had, in

exchange for money and trust, improved me—or at least, left me feeling improved. They were a constant in the wide world, from impoverished villages to the richest cities. Women visited somebody to straighten their curls, to paint their nails vibrant colors, to apply henna, or to thread off the fine, downy hair above their lip. Finally: in a new form, the familiar.

Marta was a relative stranger at first, but our time together was natural. It gave me some semblance of my old life, where I had taken pride in being buffed and manicured. Mostly, I liked to sink into the sheet, wrapped in a nubby white towel, and be cared for to the tones of Enya, Marta's hands massaging oil onto my chest or rubbing cream onto my face or holding my fingers as she shaped my nails.

She told me that she read books constantly (*The Curious Incident of the Dog in the Night-Time*—*Lo strano caso del cane ucciso a mezzanotte,* in Italian—for example) and that she worked five days a week in a spa in Orvieto and one day a week here, saving her money for her future family. She told me about friends who had slighted her and her dream of opening her own salon, and, with a sly smile, admitted that pedicures were her favorite treatment to perform because she could peel off layers of hideous skin to reveal beautiful feet, which caused women to rejoice.

Sometimes her little sister Clara was allowed to observe, if she kept silent. She sat very stiffly on the love seat, watching rapt, memorizing every step that Marta took, so that someday she, too, might become a beautician.

Soon, Marta and I began taking tea together. *Un bel tè,* she called it. Tea wasn't popular in the land of *caffè,* but Marta had received a set of holistic remedy teas from a client, and we made our way through each brightly colored packet, which bore a long explanation of the flavor's benefits (relaxation, healing, rejuvenation).

She drove us in her tidy navy Renault, shifting dramatically on the curving roads, to Todi, where she taught me how to shop thriftily, how to hit up the discount shop before I hit up the highbrow Coop. We talked about Emanuele's defects. She told me about his ex-girl-friend, who had a heavy ass and was a mama's girl.

She confessed that when she had left Ettore—the hardest thing she'd ever done—she'd played him a song by the raspy-voiced rocker Gianna Nannini, who crooned, "L'amore è bello solo se lo fai con me." Love is beautiful only when you make it with me. When the song played in her car, Marta sat up straighter; she was impressed with herself for taking a stand. And, more important, she had emerged from the trial, from the year away from him, victorious. He had come crawling back to her, and this time he was serious. She had dated another local boy in the interim.

"Bello, bravo, intelligente . . . but he was not Ettore," she conceded.

When Marta and Ettore reconciled and finally moved in together, they rented a cheap apartment in Morruzze, where Emanuele and I had kept our lovers' quarters during my initial summer stay. The place was accessed by a narrow alleyway, under an arch and up a flight of steps. It was a cramped spot, with a kitchenette, a blindingly blue bathroom that we called l'acquario, and a bedroom with maroon car-peted closets lining the walls from floor to ceiling. The ugly bedroom with its carpeted walls looked out at a shocking pastoral panorama of untouched Umbrian green, but Marta and Ettore, like most Italians, kept the heavy wooden shutters closed to control the temperature. With a fire burning in the small kitchen fireplace, Marta cooked wild boar the way Serenella had taught her, and told me about her visit to San Francisco with her sister Veronica. Marta, unlike Ettore, was adventurous; she hoped to travel to Thailand and New York and Ireland; she wanted to go to museums, to speak English, to look at architecture.

"But Ettore wants to fish and ride horses," she said. "Va bene."

She washed Ettore's clothes and taught me how to iron. She was precise in her movements, with a body as controlled as a dancer's, and with the particular strength of a woman raised by her father in the countryside. Her home was meticulous and underdone; she woke at seven in the morning and returned at seven in the evening, and refused to spend a penny more than necessary.

We stood in her kitchen, her ironing board balancing between the table and the counter, and she showed me how to run the hot metal across a T-shirt, how to press the button to let out a rush of steam, how to hold flat the sleeve. Ettore had stacked the wood neatly by the fireplace, and Marta was cooking his favorite dish on the stovetop; Marta's devotion to this life was clear. She shared this quality with Serenella: softness and warmth, paired with a fierce undercurrent that threatened to surface if anyone imperiled that which she held dear. Marta would still have put her hand in the fire for Ettore.

I wanted to want the life that Marta was aiming for. Her happiness was a result of her perspective—she desired no more than what she could reasonably have—which meant that if I could alter my perspective, I, too, could live that life. What if I whittled down my choices, as they had been whittled down for Marta?

I learned to iron and to make meatballs. But no matter how many crisp shirts I folded, I could not convince myself that folding crisp shirts was important to me. In fact, the more I tried to change, the more resistant to change I became.

Perhaps it would have been different if I had been with someone else, though a quick scan of the fellows of Collelungo led me to believe not. An older Italian woman, the wife of the baker the next town over, marveled at my presence in the area, shaking her head and announcing that I was not meant for this life. Every time she saw me, she regarded me with warm pity and wondered aloud if I'd had enough. Only an Italian woman, she claimed, could handle an Italian man. At first, I denied it. She was a know-it-all. Had I had enough? Hardly! Could I handle an Italian man? With ease, *signora*!

False.

As the baker's wife said: For the most part, only an Italian woman can handle an Italian man.

Because Emanuele was forgetful, he lost his wallet twice a year. Twice a year, he had to cancel his single credit card, shrug off the cash that had disappeared, apply for a new driver's license, and purchase a new wallet. Had he been riding a tractor, and had it slipped from his pocket into the overgrown field? Or had it fallen from the car in a parking lot anywhere from Terni to Perugia? We scoured the apartment. Finally, three days after the initial disappearance, we discovered the wallet in the trash can. Emanuele and I rejoiced. Fabio shook his head disapprovingly at his wife.

"It's your fault," he said to her.

"You're right," Serenella said.

I looked from one to the other. "How is it Serenella's fault?"

"Because if she had gone up to your house to look for the wallet, she would have found it," Fabio said. "Then, Emanuele wouldn't have had to spend so many days looking for it."

"*Scusa,* but Emanuele is thirty years old," I said. "The fact that he lost his wallet for three days is his mother's fault?"

"No, he's right. It is my fault," Serenella said, lighting her slim 100.

"She should have looked for it," Fabio said, puffing on *il sigaro infinito.*

"Look, Fabio," Serenella said, "now we've caused Giustina to turn red in the face!"

"Calma, Giustina, calma," Fabio said as I sputtered.

Even if I could miraculously convince myself to truly care about ironing and meatball making, and even if I could, say, come to enough compromises with Emanuele to sustain a happy rustic life—even then, I did not know how I would ever be able to be the good wife, if being the good wife meant one day calmly accepting blame from my husband for my grown son's lost wallet.

9

GIUSTINA, WE DON'T EAT FOR HUNGER!

—FABIO CRUCIANI

IN COLLELUNGO, EVERYTHING WAS FERTILE, and all animals and humans seemed to be perpetually reproducing. The townspeople procreated profusely, or maybe it was just that there were so
few of them that it seemed that someone was always pregnant. The
idea of having a child was practically sacred, so inherent was it to
happiness.

"I should get Marcus sterilized," I once remarked absently at
the dinner table.

"Sterilized?" asked Ettore. "She's a beautiful dog. We must
mate her."

"We could make a lot of money," Emanuele said. "You could
sell pointer puppies to all the hunters around."

"You cannot sterilize a dog," Fabio said, his eyes pained. "She
will become hysterical."

Marcus lay in her favorite sun spot in the front garden. Her
front paws were crossed, giving her the look of a proper lady.

"Hysterical?" I asked.

"Hysterical pregnancy," Fabio said. "She will so desire babies that she will imagine that she has had them. She will spend all day searching for these imagined babies until she goes insane."

"Dio mio," I said. "Are you sure?"

Fabio nodded with conviction.

"She'll produce milk, too," Ettore said.

"You are making this up," I said.

"More important," said Fabio, "your dog must make love to have a full life."

"That's ridiculous," I said. "You people were about to let this dog die."

"If she has a poopy, she will be happy," Emanuele said to me in stilted English, as if to better explain.

"It's important that you pronounce it *puppy*," I said.

"Eh, beh," Fabio said. "We used to have a dog who would run off whenever she was in heat, run to a dog down the road, and we wouldn't see her for days. One day, my father found her in a field of flowers, making love with another dog for hours, a smile on her face. Un cane deve fare l'amore."

"Un cane deve fare l'amore," the others echoed.

"How can you deny her the chance to make love?" said Fabio.

"Every creature deserves the pleasure," Serenella said.

"A female dog must be allowed to have babies," Alessandra said.

"What did you do with all the puppies?" I asked.

"We gave them away, mostly," Ettore said. "But once in a while, if we couldn't find them a place, I just suffocated them in the woods as they were born."

"It was a shame," Fabio said, looking sincerely depressed.

THAT WAS LIFE AND DEATH and love on Via Todi. It didn't make any sense at all. The Crucianis raised sheep, which they adored, despised, and ate. They used the sheep for everything the sheep could give: milk, wool, lambs. The sheep were Fabio's wards, and as such, were a tattered bunch. They slept on layers of filthy hay in one of two run-down barns and were ravaged by enormous black ticks. Their curdled, earthen smell rose up yards from where they lay, pushing me back a step each time I ventured near. These sheep were completely disorganized and followed me everywhere, illuminating for me the phrase "like sheep." I would often find myself walking through a field and when I looked behind would see fourteen long-faced, cross-eyed creatures staring at me.

"What do you want from me?" I asked the herd. "I am not your leader."

"The sheep is the world's stupidest animal," Emanuele said.

Left to its own devices, the herd was prone to eating Serenella's roses. The sheep sidestepped up to the house while Fabio, their errant shepherd, was distracted by Francesco.

"Bucala bucala bucala," he cooed at the baby, gurgling in his bouncy seat, as the sheep realized their dreams of consuming high-quality rose petals.

"O, dai, dai!" Serenella screamed, running from the kitchen at the fugitive sheep dining on her bushes. "Fabio!" She stood grumbling at the stripped, thorny branches as Fabio serenely raised himself from the couch and strolled outside. They had won prizes, those roses.

The sheep also had the habit of sneaking off through the field up to the neighbor's olive trees and feasting, so that Fabio often had to make a labored, largely futile dash up the hill to shoo them away. They also imperiled themselves and passing motorists by wandering onto the curving streets and standing there, bewildered, accidentally suicidal, as cars swerved around them.

"Che rompicoglioni, che stupidi!" Fabio said, carrying his wooden staff about. The sheep obeyed his commands, running nervously away.

The sheep were also impossible to milk, which may or may not be normal for sheep.

"Well, would you let a stranger grab your breast and pull?" Emanuele asked.

At first, Emanuele and Serenella tried to milk the sheep themselves, but it always ended badly. It took them an hour to corner a single ewe. The high jinks were out of some old-fashioned slapstick—slipping, falling, hopping up again. Emanuele, in mud-caked tennis shoes and a rain slicker, attempted to mount the ewe, under the impression that he could somehow control it from atop, while Serenella followed with a bucket, reaching out her hand toward its teats. The frightened ewe bucked Emanuele off, throwing him into piles of muck, and the sloppy dance began again.

"You'd think it would be easier," he said, wiping mud from his cheek.

"I'm calling Giamo," Serenella said, and walked back to the house.

Giamo, a Macedonian who lived two towns over, was Fabio's sole employee and could often be spotted lugging firewood bundles around the farm or driving the enormous blue diesel truck at ten miles per hour or pushing a horse into its stable. Though only forty, Giamo had the deeply lined face of someone who had experienced true poverty. He was violently strong, had very long limbs, and wore a perfect brown mullet. He could harvest fruit, cut trees, build sheds, load supplies. He lived in a rambling rental on the outskirts of nearby Vagli with his wife and shy young daughters, spoke rough, fast Italian, and could scale a hill in under ten seconds.

When Giamo arrived, the herd huddled in the corner of their pen. They knew the man was no novice. Giamo had grown up milking sheep and was widely considered somewhat of a milking maestro. For his efforts at the Cruciani farm, he was promised two wheels of aged cheese and some fresh ricotta.

Emanuele separated a ewe from the herd and rushed her toward Giamo. As the ewe ran at him, Giamo flung himself and landed on her back, sticking his feet to the ground and immobilizing the ewe between his thighs. He bent himself over her butt, reached for her udder, pushed a bucket beneath, and massaged the milk out of her. The sheep surrendered, standing limply, looking away.

"Once you control them, they have no will," Giamo said happily. "Want to try, Joos-tine?" He flashed a crooked grin.

"Dio mio, no," I said from a distance. I believed that I could still die happy without having pulled milk from the fleshy udder of one of Fabio's sheep.

Each sheep took Giamo no more than three minutes, start to finish, and soon the buckets overflowed with warm liquid that smelled of grass and dirt. Serenella lugged them into the house and spent several weeks standing over a steaming pot. In the pot, she boiled the milk until it was clean and then added a bottled solution—"made from calf intestine," she explained—to force the milk to separate into small curds and liquid whey. Then she drained the curds, added salt and sometimes rosemary, and forced them into a round mold, which she covered with a paper towel and stored in the refrigerator, changing the towel daily until the wheel had hardened. Some cheese, we ate immediately, and they were mellow and mild. Others, we ate months later, and they were strong and tart. Serenella always reboiled the leftover whey until it separated again into fresh curds that became delicate ricotta, which we sprinkled with sugar and ate warm for dessert every night.

G~J

"MILKING SHEEP IS AN ACQUIRED skill," Giamo said proudly when he collected the cheese he had been promised. "In Macedonia, we had to milk five hundred sheep a day."

The sheep, it was true, were difficult for an amateur to handle.

I figured I didn't have to worry about them. I still didn't understand that as long as you were on the farm, you were responsible for everything.

One afternoon, I stood among the olive trees at the top of the sloping meadow high with yellow grass. Marcus was exploring the area, black ears flipped back, nose pressed to the ground, running in circles, following a scent. She and I had begun to move in tandem: For every step I took, she ran in a quarter-mile circle around me. It worked well for us. A hundred yards away, by the barn with the metal roof, stood Fabio in a bright purple sweater, hollering, his hands in the air.

After some squinting, I realized that he was shouting, "Le pecore!"

The sheep. Fabio wanted me to bring him his sheep, which were, presumably, behind me, where he was motioning. I swung around to find the herd huddled together, wearing expressions of near-religious devotion. Their brows were furrowed; they craved direction. I felt at once unexpectedly important and bogged down by the responsibility. I was the unprepared de facto chief of this extremely woolly cult. They were my minions, my disciples. From across the meadow, Fabio beckoned us.

"Listen," I said to the sheep. They cocked their heads in unison. I stepped forward and they stepped back. "Go to your house," I said, flapping my hand.

The sheep stood still. I looked over at Fabio. He opened his arms wide and mimed a slow-motion lunge. I tried to imitate him, but I was too quick, too forceful. Shepherding is not best learned on the spot, and especially not from an instructor standing at a great, muted distance. The sheep, shocked by the ferocity of my movement, split into three emotional groups, scattering. Fabio threw his hands in the air. I took off after the bunch running for the dense forest. I had only wanted to fall in deep, unyielding love with a handsome gardener, I reflected as my feet slid back and forth in my galoshes.

When that hadn't gone as planned, I'd just hoped to adopt a dog. And now, I wished only to go for a stroll in the Umbrian countryside with that animal, so why, exactly, was I tumbling down the ever-steeper slope of an overgrown meadow? I was from New England! This was not in the plan! As I began a sideways jump down into the wooded area, I reflected on the fact that I had once been convinced that there actually *was* a plan. The sheep would teach me yet.

FOR ALL THEIR TRESPASSES, FOR all their forbidden feedings and debacles, the sheep were adored. Fabio doted on them, checking their food and water, securing them at night, grazing them during the day, falling ill with sorrow if one died, rejoicing when one was born. At one point, I found a long cut on Marcus's front leg and traced it back to a bloom of messily attached razor wire that suddenly surrounded the sheep entrance and exit to the field.

"To keep them from escaping to their deaths," Fabio said, when I located him in the wine cellar.

"It's too dangerous for Marcus," I said, and Fabio and I walked over to survey his work.

The sheep stood glumly at the wire.

"They're hardly vicious beasts," I said. "Regular wire would do." The sheep looked at us.

I had made a short but persuasive argument. We took some clippers from the kitchen. Serenella followed us down and shook her head at Fabio's sheep protection scheme as he made futile attempts to cut the metal. His hand kept slipping, and finally Serenella grabbed the clippers from him, pressed down, and dismantled the fence in under five minutes.

"He's too attached to the damn sheep," Serenella said that evening at dinner.

"I heard that when the shepherds stayed up in the mountains, sometimes they would make love to their sheep," I said.

"Ha," Fabio said. "But a sheep is certainly a nice, gentle animal."

"I could see how you could fall in love with a sheep," Emanuele said. "No back talk."

I strained. "A sheep?"

"Of course," Ettore said. "It happens all the time."

"Think about it: You're a shepherd, up in the hills, away from your wife, lonely," said Fabio. "You get to know a lovely little sheep. A pretty little sheep. And then one night . . ."

"You're saying it's okay to love a sheep?" I asked in awe.

"I'm saying," Fabio clarified, "I'm saying, I *understand.*"

"Seriously?" I asked. "Seriously?"

"Che stupida!" Serenella said. "Goodness, Giustina, we are country people, sure, but we are not fucking our livestock!"

The table erupted into laughter.

⌒

"È LA COSA PIÙ DOLCE," the family admitted when the lambs were born. Sheep may be an unattractive bunch, but there is nothing sweeter than a lamb. For months into the spring, the sheep grew rounder, heavier, their bellies swinging toward the ground, their udders swollen. And then, in the span of two weeks, all the lambs emerged. They came in succession, every day a new one or two. They were tiny, perfect, with soft little hooves and downy wool, in black and white and brown, with dark and pink noses. They bleated, whined, stumbled about, staying close to their mothers, who morphed from submissive followers into ferocious protectors who sat next to their newborns, glaring even at Fabio. He was especially taken by the babies and often leaned against a tree, hands in pockets, just to watch them frolic.

Over four months, we saw them grow from minuscule, shaky infants to confident young ones. They wandered away from their mothers and took to chasing each other through the fields, hopping up and down on their skinny legs, running around, chasing one another. Marcus watched hopefully from the sidelines as they cavorted. They were about her size and had the same docile character; surely, to her, they seemed like ideal playmates. But if she tried to join them, she found herself stared down by the head ewe, who put her face just inches from Marcus's and glowered. Marcus threw herself on the ground, trembling, and looked around for rescue.

"That's just embarrassing," Serenella said.

The other ewes, thrilled that a creature in the world might be frightened of them—and not the usual vice versa—ganged up, all standing boastfully behind their leader and glaring until Marcus slunk away.

"Don't be dejected," I implored her. "They're losers."

But who wouldn't want to play with the lambs? Marcus returned daily to pine for the friends denied to her.

One day in spring, I found Fabio puttering nervously around the front of the house, wearing his red rain slicker, rumpled corduroys, and scuffed-up deck shoes. He shook his head and paced across the driveway and back. Then he took a seat on the lawn chair, puffing slowly on *il sigaro infinito*. Today was the slaughter of the lambs.

"È brutto," he said. "Bruttissimo."

"But he's a shepherd," I said to Emanuele. "Isn't this what he does?"

Fabio couldn't kill his livestock, despite having been born and raised on a farm. In the winter, he mated his herd, all fertile ewes impregnated so that they would bear male lambs that he could kill for meat, or females to sell or keep as the next generation. But when the lambs were born, he loved them. He tended to them, admired them, remarked upon their beauty. And when the inevitable day came, as it did annually, his heart broke.

Meanwhile, I watched the scene with what would have been childish wonder had it not been connected to bloodletting. When

I was eleven, my mother had taken me to a sanctuary in the mountains of California, having become enamored of the calming practice
of Zen Buddhism. (When she raised her voice at me, I'd yell back,
"Yeah, that's real *Zen* of you!") There, when not soaking in the sul-
furous hot springs, the guests ate from a creative menu of vegetarian
dishes. When I returned home, I swore off meat and didn't touch the
stuff for the next thirteen years, until one day while walking through
the streets of New York, I was struck by an overwhelming desire for
a cheeseburger.

"I've never felt better," I announced after finishing off a quarter-
pounder in front of a wide-eyed friend.

Still, my relationship with meat was relatively new, tentative.
I was feeling my way, choosing well-done burgers, chicken breast,
roast turkey, grilled salmon. I hadn't gone full force—no rare porter-
house or pork sausage, no true acknowledgment of flesh. And now,
suddenly, I was learning the most gruesome details, and I didn't
avert my eyes.

Fabio called his sons and nephews over. Each lamb was separated from the herd, bleating. Emanuele held each creature down, its
eyes covered by a cloth and its feet bound, and Ettore stuck a knife
in its slim throat—in, out. The lamb twitched and gasped. Emanuele
looked away, up at the trees, keeping his hand on the lamb to hold it
down. Ettore did not look away until the lamb stopped moving.

"My father can never do it," Emanuele said. "He can't kill anything."

"Sono nati per morire," Fabio said. They are born to die. His
eyes were red.

The lamb's small body was stretched on a rack by the pigpen and
skinned, head to foot, two deep pink pieces. Then it was sold whole to
the market, where it would be butchered, wrapped in waxed paper,
and taken home by a family for dinner. Almost all the Cruciani lambs
met such a fate one by one, and the mother ewes seemed confused by

their dwindling brood. If they were particularly upset, Fabio gave them a lambskin, so they could smell their offspring again.

"No mother has an easy time losing its child," Fabio said.

HE WAS SIMILARLY ATTACHED TO his pigs. Two piglets arrived every six months, carried in the brawny, hairy arms of the pig farmer down the road. He delivered a pair of round, dark creatures with stubby legs and small, fleshy snouts.

"La porchetta è arrivata," Fabio informed me excitedly. He had found that I was the only one who would react with vigor to his farm news. The rest of the family tended to level him with a stare, as if to question how, after sixty years, he could remain excited about two pigs that would soon be dinner.

The little *porchette* began their existence at the farm pressed together, terrified, in their pen. But they soon learned to recognize Fabio as the bearer of food, and upon seeing him would run in celebratory bursts. They were quick learners, communicative, and spirited. Each day, Fabio brought them a heavy broth of leftovers: stale bread soaked in hot, soupy water, with the leaves of carrots and old lettuce, the dregs of spaghetti, tomato sauce, and bits and pieces of eggplant and squash. The pigs vigorously consumed their meal and waited until Fabio's return, when they would squeal with happiness. Within six months, they had grown from piglets the size of terriers to gigantic beasts, pushing three hundred pounds. They snorted and breathed heavily and rolled around, their hairy bodies writhing.

"I thought pigs were pink, like in the cartoons," I said. "You know, cute."

"No, not like Babe," Emanuele said.

When the pigs were a year old, they were ready to become prosciutto. Fabio put on his red rain slicker and called his cousin over. The cousin, who lived up the road with his wife, was a pig killer if ever there was one. Tall, with a heavy belly, a mass of gray hair, and thick features, he hiked proudly down to the farm, wearing a white cotton smock and rubber boots, carrying a bolt pistol and a bevy of knives and hatchets. The only phrase he knew in English was "fuck you," and he liked to say in Italian, every time he saw me, "Don't say 'fuck you' to me, because I know what it means!" Then he laughed heartily.

As he and Ettore approached the unsuspecting pig, Fabio slumped up near the house, his face drawn and childlike, on the brink of tears.

The slaughter was organized business, and the two men reminded me of a team of movie gangsters—methodical and stone cold. A pig is an immense living being, and its flesh makes it oddly reminiscent of a human; its execution is therefore especially gruesome.

"Nato per morire," Fabio said, to calm himself. "Nato per morire."

I stood to the side, covering my eyes. I peeked out from between my middle and index fingers.

First, the cousin shot the pig in the forehead with his bolt gun. It seemed humane to stun the animal, but it was mostly to keep the pig calm and to prevent it from releasing the fear-induced shot of adrenaline that makes the meat tougher, less delicious. Marcus watched from the side of the building, half of her face poking out from behind the cement, at once terrified of being the next to go and envious of their ability to kill such a big hunk of meat.

Next, Ettore and the cousin tied the pig by its massive legs, disorienting it, and led it to a rocky area outside the horse barn. Ettore held it down as the cousin brandished a large, sharp knife, placed it on the soft underside of the pig's limp throat, and drew it cleanly across. Death was not merciless, nor was it instant: The pig let out a series of gurgles and gasps as its eyes went still, and blood gushed to the ground, pooling on the dirt in bright scarlet puddles.

Ettore and the cousin looked energized. Their chests rose as they

stood above the body, triumphant, and they called Emanuele and
Paolo for help hoisting the pig onto a hook in the barn. There the late
pig hung and was rinsed with pots of boiling water, scrubbed with
soap, and rinsed again. Finally, the cousin, with whom I would not
like to be caught in a dim alleyway, drew a sparkling, foot-long single-
blade razor, shaved the dark hair off the pig, washed it again, and cut
open its stomach. He pulled out a mass of bloody entrails, threw them
into a plastic bucket, and lowered the pig from the hook.

In the kitchen, Serenella waited coolly with a cleaver. She had
set a plastic drop cloth on the dining room table, where she and the
cousin would begin the butchering. Outside, Marcus danced in the
pig blood, reddening her snout and leaving a trail of bloody paw
prints all over the farm.

That evening, I watched the plastic surgery reality show *Dr.
90210*. As the surgeon carved up a Beverly Hills tummy tuck patient,
I leaned in. He lifted a pink slab of excess skin and placed it on a
nearby scale. This was strangely, horribly familiar.

"Siamo carne!" I screeched. We're meat!

Emanuele turned to me with a puzzled look. "Certo," he said.
"What did you think we were?"

ANYTHING THAT COULD BE SHOT or picked was superior to
what could be purchased. Love, energy, and tradition produced
superior food. Raise a pig with love and kill it with respect and
you'll have a tasty pork chop for supper—a pork chop that tastes
like Collelungo.

I had figured that I might be unable to eat meat after watching
the killings, but there was a sense to those lives here; the pig was
raised to make me dinner, and it lived a pretty fine pig life and died
a pretty quick pig death, and I knew everything it had eaten, and I
had touched the plot of land it lolled about in. Instead of putting me

off, the slaughter convinced me of the importance of seeing how your meat is raised, how it dances for joy when you bring it bread, how it steals the neighbor's olives and grazes in a clean field.

Vegetables were best from the garden as well. But the Collelungese nursed a particular passion for foraging. During the fall, when mushrooms sprouted in the dank woods, the Collelungese entered a fever. Cars were abandoned by the side of the road in any area rich with mushrooms. At the bar, mushrooms were the number one conversation topic. In the home, mushrooms dominated every meal.

"It's mushroom mania," I said in English. Emanuele liked the phrase.

Mushroom mania: It sounded exotic to me—the deep forest, the *funghi* sprouting from the ground, hidden but there for the taking. It would be spectacular to traverse the unknown area like a real Italian, spotting the earthen porcini camouflaged against the dirt. Incorrect: When you don't know what you're doing, turns out mushroom hunting is a real drag.

One day in October, I rode with Emanuele in the rattling backseat of Ettore's Fiat Panda through the dirt roads of a nearby village and into a field. Marta and Ettore sat stoically in the front, their faces grave and focused. Before I knew what was happening, we were running in silence through a wildflower field, Ettore several strides ahead, with one hand motioning for us to hurry, the other placed on his mouth in the universal hush sign.

"We're not allowed here?" I whispered to Emanuele as I jogged.

"He just doesn't want anyone to see us and know where the good mushrooms are," Emanuele whispered back.

When we entered the dim forest, we found dozens of other foragers tiptoeing about, many in what seemed like mushroom-collecting outfits: brown hats, high socks. They wore mushroom sacks across their chests and scanned the ground in utter concentration. Some looked at us, irritated at yet another person in on the good spot; some tipped their heads in a silent greeting.

"Be careful of vipers," Emanuele said and took off.

I didn't need him! With my trained journalistic eye, my street smarts, and my powers of perception, I was going to be awesome at this little game.

At the end of the hour, we all met up. In my concentrated wanderings, I had found exactly three mushrooms, sprouting up camouflaged against the dirt. Mostly, I had devoted my energies to not getting eaten by a viper. Emanuele had found twenty-five. Ettore was scraped, sweating, and bleeding, having shinnied up hills, below bushes, into thickets where only rabbits could go. Marta's deep black curls were tangled, her face dirty. Together, she and Ettore had found two hundred voluptuous forest mushrooms. They had beaten their record of a hundred fifty from the previous day. Marta regarded me with shrouded compassion. I smiled wanly in return.

That night, the Cruciani household was piled high with mushrooms. Serenella stood at her counter, elbow deep in porcini, in *funghi selvaggi*. Over the next several days, she preserved mushrooms, sliced, in jars with oil, vinegar, and herbs, dried them on a long string over the fire, and cooked them with pasta and polenta.

"Mushroom mania," Paolo said in English, walking past her projects. Emanuele had spread the phrase around town.

IN SPRING, THE LOCALS WENT similarly nuts for the wild asparagus growing in thatches all around. The asparagus stalks were skinny and pungent, deeply flavored, and the Collelungese wandered the fields and streets with long clippers specifically made for asparagus. I walked with Serenella for hours, seeing only shoots of tall grass where she saw, ever accurately, a bounty of *asparagi*.

"And here is a crop," she said, pointing at an indiscernible sprout of grass. She pushed it aside to reveal twenty asparagus.

"I saw nothing," I said. "How did I see nothing?"

"It takes years to train the eye," she said. "Non ti preoccupare."

Usually, Serenella catered to her family's subtle tastes, adding the asparagus to pasta. But since she knew I was enamored of the stuff and that I wanted it all, tons of it, without the distraction of penne, she often made me my own bowl, sautéed with olive oil and garlic. She did the same with field *cicoria,* a light, leafy green that she picked at the American art dealer's house; he wanted nothing to do with his accidental crop, so Serenella greedily cleaned him out and arrived back with armfuls of the stuff, shaking her head in wonder at his willingness to let it go.

"Calma, calma," Fabio said to me as I inhaled the vegetables, which delighted me and depressed me at once—I now knew that this was how asparagus actually tasted, and the difference between the dense, delicate stuff and the watery, chewy stalks from Stop n' Shop was the difference between a perfectly ripe cherry and the corn syrup pellet we call cherry-flavored candy. "Ti fa male!" It will make you ill.

THERE WERE OTHER CULINARY SURPRISES.

"Buon giorno," Serenella muttered one afternoon, a long, thin cigarette hanging from her mouth. She sat by the door, her arm inside a burlap sack that was resting on her lap.

"Buon giorno," I said. I'd come down to help clean up before lunch.

"You like pigeon?" Serenella asked with a smile.

Piccione—pigeon. It's difficult for a New Yorker to really like pigeons, "rats with wings," as they are known in the five boroughs: those gray and blue creatures, flying above the city and painting it with their excrement, walking haughtily along the sidewalk, eating leftover french fries. I had eaten a pigeon once before at the Crucianis, though, and it had, admittedly, been quite succulent. Sure, I liked pigeon. Why?

The burlap sack began to rustle. "Hmm," said Serenella, puffing on the cigarette. Then she steadied the bag with one hand and twisted her arm sharply. The sack stopped rustling. She pulled from it a slate-colored bird, its broken neck tucked neatly down, and placed it on the table next to her.

"Pigeon is for dinner," she said.

"Pigeon it is," I said.

Each bird was plucked, skewered, and roasted over an open fire until the skin was crisp and salty.

"You don't like it, you can get the hell out," Alessandra said.

"Really?" I asked. I'd begun to take everything literally. "In that case, I love it."

"No, I'm kidding!" Alessandra said. "But it really is *buonissimo*."

Meanwhile, Marta was scavenging everyone's plate for salted pigeon brains.

A few days later, Emanuele watched a pair of homing pigeons fly through the sky. "What beautiful pigeons," he said.

"They are beautiful," I said. "Graceful."

"So graceful I would like to buy them," Emanuele said, "and then kill them."

The town hunters also liked sparrows, rabbits, and wild boar. I once watched Ettore wander by Nonna Ferrina's house.

"O, Ettore, che fai?" she yelled from her permanent position leaning halfway out the window. Hey, Ettore, whatcha doin'?

"O, Nonna," he said, reached into his pocket, pulled out a dead sparrow, and tossed it at her. She caught it with one hand.

But sparrow hunting and rabbit hunting had nothing on boar hunting, which attracted the more brutally masculine Collelungo bunch. The boars, *i cinghiali,* rumbled through the woods in packs, so that the hunters, usually outfitted in full camouflage, could stand with rifles in wait and then kill them in groups. The hunters left early in the morning with their guns slung over their arms, and they hunched, smoking and whispering, in the brush for hours, hoping for a boar to wander into their midst. When it happened, they arrived drunk on success at the village bar, their crumbling pickups stuffed with seven or eight dead black boars, covered in coarse fur, their round, fleshy snouts dripping with blood, their bodies sticky and smeared crimson, with a forlorn boar-sniffing dog, its own muzzle tinged red, its ears drooping low, chained up next to them in back. Then all winter, the wives and girlfriends cooked boar stew, its meaty tomato sauces to be sponged up by bread.

But in the end, pigeon and boar and asparagus, however exciting, were complements to the adored troika of necessities: wine, bread, and olive oil.

"UMBRIA HAS THE FINEST WINE land in all of Italy," Fabio contended. "This is the only stuff that won't make you ill." When he went out to eat once a year, he spit out bottled wine. "Velenoso," he said. Poisonous. Once, I brought him a bottle of excellent Barolo, and he looked at it with disdain as he sipped his own tannic creation.

"Be careful, my father's wine will give you a two-day headache," Emanuele whispered. Ettore and Nonno Renato, who were made of strong stuff, drank it by the gallon, though everyone else mixed it with a generous amount of sparkling water. It was a sweet, simple table wine with an overfermented, bubbly quality.

"It's restaurant wine that gives you a headache," Serenella said. "All chemicals."

Cruciani wine was made from the fruit of the twisted ancient vineyard across the street, where Fabio tended to indigenous vines. During the spring, he enlisted the help of his entire family to slowly pick each and every bunch of grapes from the untended vines. He hand-pressed the grapes and allowed them to ferment naturally in barrels, giving us some of *il mosto*—the sweet liquid before it became alcoholic. Then he aged the wines in his makeshift wine cellar, a cool, cobweb-thick concrete room next to the sheep barn. Once the wine was ready, Fabio ambled down every few days and filled up his glass bottle with red or white.

"Umbria is wine country," he said.

"Not really," I said; the New York businessman whose memoirs I was writing was teaching me about fine wines. "Piedmont is wine country."

"Nope, it's a fact that Umbria has the best soil for wine," Fabio said.

"How is it a fact?"

"Because it is," he said.

The only thing worse than Fabio's wine was Umbrian bread. Bread, globally: flour, water, yeast, and salt. Bread in Umbria: flour, water, yeast. In the sixteenth century, the Vatican imposed a high tax on salt, and the regions of Tuscany and Umbria revolted. They would make their bread without salt. Even when salt was no longer exorbitantly expensive, the Umbrians kept making their bread thus: Each lacking loaf was white, with a light yellow crust, flavorless, and strangely textured. It turned rock-hard within a day. The entire cuisine was heavily salted to compensate for the bread's shortcomings.

"This bread is not very good," I said one evening, expecting a backlash.

"What a waste of money," Serenella agreed. Every day, they purchased two loaves of bread, and usually a portion went bad. "No flavor."

"Turns into stone in twelve hours," Fabio grumbled. "Feed it all to the pigs."

"That Calabrian bread at the market in Todi is excellent," Emanuele added. "Crusty, delicious."

The Coop in Todi sold salted bread, and the bakery in the next town over had a limited supply of salted baguettes. But the local bakery made only the classic loaves.

"So—nobody likes this stuff?" I asked, holding up a piece.

"Who would like it?" Serenella asked. "It's no good without sauce."

"But everybody buys it every day?"

"Certo," she said with a nod.

"Why don't you just change the type of bread you eat, then?" I scanned the room.

"We couldn't," Emanuele said.

"But nobody likes it?"

"Not really."

"So why can't everyone demand a different type of bread?"

The family stared at me with puzzled expressions on their faces.

"Eh, beh," Fabio finally said. The next morning, the quotidian loaves arrived on the table, left there by the bakery delivery boy. That evening, we used them to wipe up the oil from the pork chops. A day later, Marcus gratefully gnawed on the stony heel.

⚬～⚬

IN NEW YORK, ARTISANAL OLIVE oil was poured onto little plates at expensive grocery stores, and customers could dip a bit of toast in it and remark on the spice. It was a Mediterranean treat, healthier than butter, more elegant than vegetable oil, lovely mixed with lemon atop salads.

In Italy, olive oil was life. Without olive oil, there would be no cuisine.

Emanuele swore he could feel the emotions of the olive trees when he trimmed their branches—in agriculture school, he had concentrated on this particular art. Fabio tended to his grove with solemn devotion, and in the fall, everyone in the family met up to begin the tedious task of olive picking.

The Cruciani olive groves started in a patch by their house, growing haphazardly, and continued on down the hills, hundreds of them, or so it seemed. On the family's steep land, where the horses grazed, the trees were planted in strict lines and rose up toward the house and down toward the road, with no end in sight. The branches grew heavy with fine, sage-colored leaves in late October and early November, when we were required to relieve them of their fruit. All down Via Todi, families were doing the same, gathered together, perched on ladders, wearing sun hats.

On the first day of the harvest, I found the family, plus Marta, standing in the kitchen decked out in stiff protective gloves, rain slickers, and boots. We marched to the first row, and I stood by as Fabio and sons laid long black nets with tiny holes beneath the trees. We picked each olive, thousands of green and brown and black orbs falling down to the ground. Sometimes, Emanuele borrowed his boss's olive picker, a sort of metal arm that shook the olives down from the highest branches. But usually, it was labor literally done by hand.

"Can I eat one?" I asked the first day, holding a black, shiny, fresh olive, plucked from the tree.

"Sure, you can try," Ettore said. Paolo stood behind him, regarding me expectantly.

I placed the olive in my mouth and spit it out: bitter, sour, dry.

"So, they don't come off the tree tasting briny and oily," I said.

"Right." The brothers used me as their own private form of entertainment.

The picking looked romantic when you walked by those lovely dusty-green groves, but it was dreadfully tedious. After three days,

I lost my gusto, retreated to the house, and tried to mop the floor to feel useful. But I wasn't useful—I was lazy. The Crucianis kept their mouths shut; they understood that I was often *egoista,* and they forgave me for it.

The rest of the group, not so faint in spirit or body, continued to harvest for weeks on end. Every day, they pulled the nets together and emptied them into heavy crates. The crates were then loaded into a friend's white, rickety 4x4 truck, which groaned down the makeshift paths, dropping the bins by the house.

Marcus rushed up and down the hill, edging closer to the group and then fleeing; sniffing them from afar and backing away. Once in a while, she grasped an olive in her mouth and carried it gingerly about. Then she laid it down, took a step back, bowed, and growled at the lone olive. It was a misguided attempt to convince the olive to play with her.

"I hate to burst your bubble . . . ," I said, leaning against a tree.

Finally, late in November, we all took turns ferrying the olives to a communal mill in the backwoods of a nearby village. The mill was located in an old barn, with metal doors and high ceilings, unheated and possibly unsanitary. There, farmers and families dropped their crops into huge forest green vats, piled high with hundreds of thousands of black and sage olives, some still attached to bits of wood and leaf.

The employees of the mill were a group of rugged fellows in coveralls and high rubber boots, who refused to crack a smile as they emptied the olives into the presses, a squalid collection of old and new technology. First, the olives were placed in a long metal contraption, where they were rinsed, freed of leaves, and dried. Then, an employee lugged them to a stainless steel roller, which crushed the olives into a paste that looked like tapenade. The paste, loaded onto a tall press, was slowly mixed with water; oil began to drip from each section being pressed, flowing down the machine's sides and into a container below. The oil was then poured into steel vats for families to take home. At the end of the process, the mill employees served us the mildly spicy golden oil fresh from the presses, drizzled on warm toast.

For a while, it was difficult for me to enjoy olive oil in any amount, so aware was I finally of the excessive effort that went into making just a teaspoonful—and of how I had not made any of that effort. But that wasn't how the Collelungese treated the stuff—they poured it everywhere and ate it all up, and they poured it on my food, too, and soon, again, so did I.

I HAD ALWAYS BEEN ONE of those people who burrow into the milk shelf in the supermarket, trying to find the most far-off date stamped on the carton. I hated dents in apples, mold on cheese. I threw out anything I suspected of being old or bad. I got the willies when food wasn't scrubbed clean, fresh from the package. I was so disconnected from my food that it kind of creeped me out: Where had it come from? When had it arrived? What was I expected to do to prepare it? Was it possible to bypass all these questions and merely acquire a hot, prekilled, precooked, prerolled box of dumplings at the stand down the street?

But in Collelungo, through all the slaughters and all the harvests, nothing was thrown out. The bones and innards of the pigs and lambs were fed to neighbors' dogs (I saved cooked leftovers for Marcus). The stale bread was fed to the pigs or fashioned into *panzanella*, a sort of savory bread pudding made with raw onions and tomatoes and olive oil, and served garnished with parsley or basil. The wine was consumed whether it was bubbly or fine, the ricotta baked into a cake, bruised tomatoes ground into sauce. Once, I held a blackened peach over the garbage can, and Fabio yelled out in a panic.

"But it's rotten," I said.

"No, it's perfectly good," he countered, grabbing it from my hand. He then proceeded to elegantly cut off each and every bad spot from the peach, leaving several pieces of juicy fruit deep below.

"Tsk," he said. "Look at this prize."

Serenella nodded. I'd seen her use brown bananas to bake a fluffy breakfast loaf.

The post-slaughter feasts included the extended family. The entire house seemed for several days to be dedicated to the pig. First it was chopped apart on the kitchen table, then further broken down, its parts packed and frozen. Its liver was cut into pieces, nestled between sage leaves, speared, and roasted over the open fire. Serenella then took the ground pork shoulder, mixed it with spices, and pressed it into the cleaned intestines, stringing dozens of sausages across the ceiling so that they would dry in the warmth of the living room. Shanks, to be used for lean prosciutto, were rubbed with salt and pepper and cured in the cellar. There was also capicola, dry-cured shoulder, fatty and smoked for six months. All over Collelungo, families were making their own cuts of pig, each clan insisting that it owned the secret to the finest hams. On picnics, for snacks, during lunch, before dinner, the Collelungese raved about their own creations and quietly sneered at those made by others.

"Secret family recipe," each of them said, giving me a slice. "Best in Collelungo, wouldn't you admit it?"

"The best," I always said.

During the first dinner after the pig was killed, we ate the fresh pork chops, sautéed lightly in olive oil, with white rice and a plain salad with lettuce, carrots, and olive oil. Really, the greens had become a dish made specifically for me, because everyone else scoffed at them.

"Salad is a waste of time," Fabio said. "You could be eating meat."

The main post-slaughter treat was *fegato,* or liver, which had been cooking on the spit for hours. It was served with the crispy sage leaves and was disastrously salty. The Crucianis ate it all, though, praising its deep, internal flavors, as I pushed it about on my plate.

The lamb feast, which came only once a year, was decidedly more elaborate. Since a lamb is smaller than a pig and vastly more expensive, the Crucianis sold most of theirs and kept only one (or two, if Ettore requested one for his birthday dinner). The lamb was usually gone within two days—roasted with herbs and served stacked high on a silver platter. The Crucianis loved it. That is, except for Fabio.

"He's not eating?" I asked Emanuele during the lamb feast. Fabio sat glumly at the end of the table, spooning *minestra* into his mouth while everyone else gleefully gorged on meat.

"No lamb," Fabio mumbled.

"You don't like it?" I asked.

"He loves lamb," Emanuele said. "But he doesn't eat his own lamb."

"My father can't," Alessandra said. "He can eat it in a restaurant or at a friend's, but not the ones he raised."

"Mai," Fabio said. Never. He shook his head and returned to his broth. The family ignored him and took seconds, all of them powering through the mountain of meat until only a delicate piece was left, the platter shiny with oil, plastered in leftover thyme and salt. Then they left the table one by one, as they did after every meal, sprawling across chairs and couches, lighting cigarettes, turning up the volume on the ever-blaring television so that we could watch the news, the soccer game, the weird bread commercial where the child sticks his index finger perversely into a steaming roll and then offers the camera a gap-toothed smile. Only Fabio remained at the table for a good half hour after the others had scattered, peeling his fruit, cutting slivers of *parmigiano,* finishing off his second cup of wine, resuming *il sigaro infinito*. He sat there, before the dishes had been cleared, and gazed at the platter, the lone, leftover lamb chop. After some time, he leaned in and picked it up, holding it between his thumb and index finger.

"Nobody will even eat this?" he asked. The family offered up a chorus of groans and resumed their postdinner activities.

"O, agnellino mio," Fabio said softly to the lamb chop. "Tutto quello, e per che cosa?"

Oh, my little lamb—all that, and for what?

I HAVE TO TRUST WHAT
WAS GIVEN TO ME
IF I AM TO TRUST ANYTHING.

—"GIFT," W.S. MERWIN

I SHARED A TABLE WITH the Crucianis, and I ate their food, but I was never really theirs. When Emanuele and I fought, he went to them, and I could not. Instead, I was left to my own devices, sitting with a telephone that called only local numbers. We fought about the same thing again and again. Though we seemed to be arguing about his tardiness and my relentlessness, we were really expressing our frustration over being mismatched on a fundamental level. Sometimes, after we fought, I walked down the hill as the sky grew deeper blue.

I saw our dented car parked outside the family house. In the dark, it was like New York: From the outside, I could watch whole lives without being seen. From the driveway, I saw Emanuele in there, his silhouette sharp in the bright lights, holding Francesco or lying on the couch with Ettore or Fabio in the glow of the television. I stood there—shifty, scared of being discovered and exposed—and watched Serenella hunched over her lacework. I could see the bright yellow refrigerator, the wine bottle on the table.

Then I headed down the slope in the dusk, past the cellar and the stable, to Marcus's pen, where she stood, tail wagging, her ears pressed tight against her glossy little head. I let her free to run in the field as the sky turned violet. At the top of the next hill was an unfinished villa, midconstruction. Nobody lived there. Outside lay the fallen trunk of a tree, and I sat upon it and looked out over the town. I could see all the lit windows of houses lining Via Todi, and Marcus sprinting in the grass. Then she flew up to me, screeching to a halt, and she pushed her soft chest into my chest and rested her head on my shoulder, panting in my ear, as the sun disappeared completely. The Crucianis had their circle, the one into which Emanuele was born. With Marcus, I felt I had at least the beginning of something just as meaningful—something that was mine, the beginning point of a circle.

"Si ama chi si ama," Fabio had said.

Late at night, when Emanuele returned and we regained a sense of order, we got into bed. In the blackness, even after a difficult day, I was grateful to have him there. But sometimes I wished that a small, spotted dog was curled up in his place.

〰️

MARCUS LIVED IN HER PEN for two months after I found her. She leaped up onto me in the mornings when I came to release her, smearing me with mud, and then took off from her cage to the field, making her loops around the land. I was teaching her to sit and to come, and I was teaching her her name.

"Just say her name a lot as you give her affection," Emanuele suggested, so I sat next to her, rubbing her ears. "Marcus, Marcus, Marcus," I repeated into her ear.

I let her run up to the olive trees and then crouched down and threw open my arms and yelled, "Vieni qua!" and Marcus came tearing at me as I encouraged her. "Brava! Brava! Bravissima!" When she arrived, I gave her a crumble of biscuit.

From her quiet, tidy house up the hill, Zia Tiziana could hear my strange, heavily accented cries of "Vieni qua." An American, bellowing in Italian, "Come here! Come here! Come here!" And then, after a moment, "Good! Good! How good! Very good!" From her window, she couldn't see the action, so she marched down to the house at lunchtime.

"What are you doing down there, Giustina?" she asked, concerned.

"She is training that *dog*," Serenella said, exasperated. She dragged on her long cigarette.

"That dog is named Marcus," I told Tiziana.

"What's the name?" Tiziana asked. Italians, it turned out, could not pronounce it.

"Maacks," said Serenella.

"No! Marquez," said Emanuele.

"I thought Mackusss," said Ettore.

"Mex?" asked Tiziana.

"Mar-*cus*," I said.

They regarded me. "Well, why did you name it that?" Tiziana asked. "Un cane si chiama Maacks. Che strano!"

⌒∿⌒

I WAS SCARED TO LEAVE Marcus outside of her pen. I thought, despite Emanuele's belief that the dog would stay put, that Marcus might run off and get lost. One night, however, once the household was asleep, a gang of unambitious robbers came again (*Albanesi! No, Russi! No, da Macedonia. No, da Romania!*) and broke into the barn. They gathered up Emanuele's guitar, some of the old furniture, and a feed bucket or two. In the morning, Emanuele's phone rang.

"I ladri," he told me, turning over in bed with an air of severity. "The thieves have struck the barn."

"And Marcus?" I asked. Had the thieves taken Marcus? Ettore
once told me, as the family nodded solemnly, that I should be careful, since Marcus was such a pretty pointer now, and hunters might
want to steal her.

We rushed down to the house to find the metal doors more
dented than usual, with the skimpy locks easily clipped through.
There hadn't been much to take. Fabio was wandering the premises
with *il sigaro infinito* hanging from his mouth, shrugging, relieved
that his sheep hadn't been harmed. Later, he set down special blades
in the ground in order to thwart others who hoped to hurt his sheep
in the deep night. Of course, I immediately drove over them, punc-
turing all four tires.

On the day of the robbery, Fabio kept muttering, "They were
here to take the sheep," and nobody could ever convince him that a
gang of thieves probably didn't want to run off with fourteen
scrawny ewes.

The ewes were fine, but Marcus was nowhere to be found. The
door to her pen hung open, and her handcrafted blue *casa* was empty.
I rushed up to the main house and then back down to her plot. My
eyes began to tear; the gypsy thieves had stolen my perfect little
pointer, and she was shaking in the back of their van, petrified.

"Marcus!" I cried out. "Vieni qua! Vieni qua! Vieni qua!"
I stood atop the hill, increasingly hysterical. "Vieni qua! Marcus!
Vieni qua!" The fields were quiet. I could see Todi, the castle, the big
empty farmhouse in the distance, the olive trees, but no dog. I hollered on until I grew hoarse, imagining my terrified animal speeding
toward the border.

Suddenly, far off in the distance, I saw a dot on the horizon. It
was like Lawrence of Arabia—the blank white sands stretching for
miles, and then, galloping ever closer, the grand steed. Marcus was
that horse, emerging from woods, a black dot in a swift, even stride,
closing in on the house.

"Brava!" I yelled, feeling my entire body open up again. "Brava, Marcus!"

She flew toward me and screeched to a halt at my feet, dust billowing up behind her. I fell to the ground and wrapped my arms around her to comfort her. Wait—Marcus did not look traumatized. Rather, she looked quite pleased, her mouth agape in a toothy grin, her long pink tongue hanging to the side, her paws covered in dirt and grass from the deep woods where she had spent the morning relishing her newfound freedom. She looked back at her big, wooded playground, clearly planning her next romp.

"The robbers let out dogs so that the dogs don't bark," Fabio explained. Then, looking at my face, he paused. "Giustina, that dog will not leave you."

"She wanted to take a little tour is all," Emanuele said.

This was how Marcus was allowed to roam free. From then on, I rarely penned her, and she rarely left the front of the house, where she claimed a square of grass by a rock, far enough from the door to feel safe but close enough to witness comings and goings. It was from this place that she waited for horses. Sometimes as I sat outside at Le Stelle bar at the edge of town, I heard the clip-clopping of hooves, and the horse and rider would appear in the distance, followed by Marcus, keeping pace, a determined look on her face.

"Che bel cane," *i vecchi* said approvingly from their chairs.

One day, she left for eight hours, following Emanuele's cousin Flavio to Todi, twenty miles away. From the outskirts of Todi, Flavio called to say that he had lost track of the dog somewhere in the backwoods and forest paths; she was with him and then she was not. At midnight Marcus showed up at the door, tapped it with her paw, and found a sympathetic figure in Serenella, who may have thought *le bestie* were disgusting, but who fed the hungry, whatever the species. Serenella gave Marcus some water and leftover spaghetti, and the delighted dog snoozed until the next afternoon.

The neighbors told me to chain Marcus or to cage her again, but I couldn't. Marcus was too happy; she seemed healthier and in better spirits than when she had spent twenty-two hours a day cooped up, and I liked to find her snoozing in a sun spot by the rosebushes. Better free and in danger than jailed and safe.

Soon, I began receiving calls in the early morning. Someone had driven by the house on a tractor, and Marcus had followed. She was pounding the streets of Izzalini. I would throw on my coat and drive, grumbling, to the village, over the narrow, sharply curving roads slicing through the mountains, to find Marcus in a lively trot down the middle of the street, on her way home. Then I'd have to screech to a halt, pulling my wheels up onto the grass, and call her. She craned her neck, stock-still on the road, and then, recognizing me, walked over and allowed me to put her in the front seat. She always looked disappointed that she could not continue her explorations as she liked, but she never resisted me. When other people stepped closer to her, she bolted, hunched to the ground, her brown eyes big wet circles of shock and fear. But she let me do with her as I wished.

WHEN I WORKED IN NEW YORK, I walked one day from my office building to the imposing tower of black glass that was the Time Warner Center at Columbus Circle. Though I was headed to the grocery store on the bottom floor to pick up some lunch, I took a moment to wander the shops, admiring the heavy canvas purses, the shining iron cookware, the mohair sweaters, lilac-scented hand creams, and gel blushes for sale at the chain stores that dotted the skyscraper. On that day, I wandered into a custom leather boutique. As I gazed into the glass at an extravagant wallet, a woman entered. She opened a tote bag, and an Italian greyhound popped out and hopped onto the counter. It was an elegant creature, weighing in at fifteen pounds, its slender silver body quivering.

"I'm here for my coat," the woman announced. She wore an intricate, claustrophobia-inducing outfit that involved a fur head wrap that obscured her hair, a turtleneck, a heavy vest, tight jeans, an ornate belt, and high, laced stiletto boots.

The coat arrived, presented by one of the salesmen. It was a small black leather motorcycle coat, studded with rocks and dripping with tassels. The woman picked up the dog and slid the leather motorcycle coat onto him.

"Mommy loves her baby," she said to the wilting creature, which was weighed down by his custom couture. "So handsome!"

How could this be? I had wondered. Now, with Marcus at my feet, I understood how dogs can drive us to do insane things. I would respect Marcus's dogginess. I would never dress her as a bumblebee for Halloween or mistake her for a baby human, but I could understand. I could understand the desire, however deranged, to express one's affection in whatever way one best knew how, even if it was wrongheaded, even if it was ego driven. One was overwhelmed with a sense of helpless love, whether it was pure or corrupt or misguided.

I had begun to sneak Marcus into the house when Emanuele was at work, and when I was away from her, I longed for her next to me, curled up neatly like a speckled egg.

"Dogs are opportunists," the people of Collelungo explained; the Italians used the word *opportunista* often to describe anybody inauthentic and political, and they always hissed it out as though it were a cardinal sin. According to the Collelungese, dogs were canine manipulators, really, and you couldn't trust them, not around children and not in your house. I could see the Italians' point about dogs working you for food, but we used them, too—to find pigeons and boars, to provide company. And then there was the small black face, sitting as I had ordered, yearning, hoping that she was always doing the right thing. "Sono la padrona di Marcus," I said out loud. I am Marcus's owner. But inside, I thought, shamefully, involuntarily, "Sono la mamma di Marcus."

OUR RELATIONSHIP SHIFTED WHEN MARCUS grew up. One evening, as I left dinner, she ran to me, frantically circling my legs and fixing me with pleading looks. I could not read her behavior, which was unusual; after dinner, when the sun had gone down, I rarely received more than a calm sniff before she retired to her *casa*, which I had finally carried up from the cage and placed beneath the olive tree by the driveway. Now she had exited her *casa* and made a small nest from a hay bale near the sheep barn. She would make several turns, lie down in the nest, and then spring up and implore me to do something, anything. I fetched a flashlight and investigated the area. I picked up her paws, looked over her body, moved the hay, and could come to no conclusion. I left her there down by the farm and drove up to the city center. I watched her anxious face in the headlights as she lay curled but alert, following my departure.

By the next morning, she had begun to bleed. She was just one year old, and I assumed it was her first period. Initially, she tried to lick the blood away but soon became accustomed to it. I, however, did not. As soon as I saw the first scarlet droplet, an image appeared in my head: my pointer, heavy with a litter, and then, suddenly, ten pups sprouting out, covered in downy hair, reaching for her teats. Covered in downy hair, and my responsibility, each and every one.

I dragged the *casa* back into the pen and ordered Marcus inside. "You're *not* getting knocked up in the backcountry," I explained, sliding the lock shut. She fixed her brown eyes on me and stood on her back legs, pressing her front paws against the fence. No matter what, Marcus never barked. I shook my head; I would have to be strong until this had passed.

A few days later, I went down in the morning to let her out and found her prancing about the front lawn.

"Who released the dog?" I asked. The cage was closed, but the dog was free.

"Nobody," Fabio said.

"Well, somebody did," I said. "She's in heat; you cannot let her out! Che cazzo!" What crap! My vocabulary was expanding to include profanities; I had also learned how to properly rest the fingers of each hand together and shake them lightly up and down to physically express the phrase "What the hell?!" as well as how to smack my left hand against the crook of my right elbow while making a righteous skyward fist with my right hand in order to physically express the phrase "Va a fare in culo!" I had studied with Marta, an expert.

Fabio shrugged. I took Marcus for her run in the pasture and then locked her in her cage. The next day, she was waiting for me by her patch of grass.

"Impossibile," I said. I had inspected the cage; there were no holes, no escape routes.

"I didn't touch it," Fabio promised. I put her away again. Twenty minutes later, she was out front, settling into her Marcus-shaped spot of tamped-down grass. I brought her back down and repeated the imprisonment. Then I headed to the main house and tiptoed over to the garage, which sat directly above Marcus's pen. From my vantage point, I watched as she pushed up a one-inch opening between the dirt and the fence, pressing the wire until it curved, giving her a total of three inches, enough for her to poke her snout out. Then, like a contortionist, she squished her head under, popped her front paw through, flattened her body to the ground, and slid out on her side. Her bones seemed to bend without breaking. Within seconds, she was greeting me like a long-lost friend and then taking off for a sniffing excursion. Her escape threw me into a panic. Male dogs had begun to break the chains to which they were tethered and hang out near the house like teenage louts, planning to pounce. They were scruffy mutts, most of them, and they had their eyes on my girl.

"Get, get!" I ordered. "She's too young for you!" They'd trot off for the moment, and then I'd see them slinking back, sniffing her heady scent in the air.

Worse, my innocent virgin was in a state herself. Her vulva had grown to three times its natural size, and it was uncomfortable to look at her from behind; she was pink and pulsating. When she saw her suitors from afar, she moved her tail to the side, hopefully. I once found a puppy on the property, attempting to penetrate her. He couldn't have been more than six months old. He had his paws balanced on her waist, but he was very short and inexperienced. He stood to her side, vehemently thrusting at the air.

"Non arriva," Fabio said, looking humiliated for the puppy.

Marcus did not reject his advances, though. She stood still and offered herself up. Meanwhile, the Italians continued to advise me to allow Marcus some action.

"Your dog must experience lovemaking just once, or what is her life?" Fabio once again insisted.

"Who will deal with the pregnant dog and all her puppies?" I asked.

"She'll naturally do all the work," Ettore said. "La mamma fa tutto." The mom does everything.

"Remember, Giustina," Fabio said from his perch on the couch, "the dog will go *mad* if she cannot have children."

"She's your dog now," Emanuele said. "You do what you think is right."

I was consumed with regret; why hadn't I gotten her spayed earlier? What had happened on those nights when she was running free? I could never know. I had enough problems with the deteriorating relationship, the cultural hiccups, the halting language. The last thing I needed was a pregnant dog. I could only pray that I would not find her with a bloated tummy once this menstrual ordeal was done.

〰

I FOUND HER WITH A bloated tummy. A few weeks after her period of heat, I noticed that her normally slender belly was taut and round. I turned her on her back and looked at the soft, rosy skin. Her teats were full. This was just my luck—now I had a pregnant dog in the middle of Umbria. I obsessed over what to do next.

"Let her have the puppies," Ettore said. "I'll . . . handle them."

"Dio mio, Ettore!" I said. He wanted to put a hit out on the unborn puppies!

The life of a dog in Collelungo was a life of misery. The animals proliferated, since the locals despised the idea of spaying and neutering. Sometimes, they would allow a female to bear a litter and then spay her, so at least she knew the supposed joy of motherhood. A male dog would never have his testicles cut off; the mere idea of subjecting any fellow—no matter the species—to such an indignity enraged the men around town. The subsequent bunches of mutts were rounded up, doled out to the farmers. Behind the bucolic village were mangy dogs living out their short lives in dirty pens. There was the wild-eyed yellow lab whose neck had grown a green ring from the metal collar attached to the stake to which he was permanently chained. There was the white fluffy watchdog attached to a tire by the compound at the bottom of the hill.

Cousin Flavio owned a gorgeous young springer spaniel named
Tina, whose long black-and-white coat glistened in the sun. She was
low to the ground, with liquid eyes and a soft, wet nose, and she was
allowed out of her cage during the day, free to follow her remarkable
sense of scent around the farm, that wet nose pressed to the ground,
letting out snorts and whimpers of glee as she tracked a deer or a
bunny. Most of the time, however, she bounced around the work-
shop where Flavio; his father, Sauro; Ettore; and a local named
Gianmaria worked in Sauro's welding business.

Tina was a gentle, fervently friendly young dog, who greeted
me by flopping on her back, offering her little pale paunch. Flavio
had raised her by the bottle and seemed torn between his accidental
love for the dog and the cultural belief that a dog was dirty. Tina had
broken loose during her cycle, and Flavio, suspecting that she may
have gotten pregnant, allowed an unqualified friend to give her an
injection in the uterus to induce miscarriage. Soon thereafter, Tina
became sluggish. Before, she could keep up with Marcus when we
went to visit, but she grew slower and less energetic, always maintaining a happy face, her sunny disposition defeating her pain. When
Flavio realized that she was ill, it was too late. He took her to the
veterinary hospital, but an infection had ravaged her insides, and
then she was dead. Tina was two years old. Flavio shook his head,
ashamed of his grief, and vowed never to own another dog.

Briefly, Marta's father toted around a tiny mongrel, the size of
his hand. The mutt accompanied him everywhere as it grew. Eventually, it reached ten pounds—a brown and black thing with dainty
paws. Once, during a birthday party for Ettore at Marta's house,
I sat on the ground outside and held the mutt to me. It lay in my
arms and accepted my scratches and caresses, falling asleep in my
lap. I often saw it running around the house, making friends with a
striped kitten, sleeping in the sun. And then, suddenly, I arrived for
my weekly facial at Marta's spa and saw the dog strung up to a short

chain that dangled from a branch. It could hardly move from its spot, despite the pounding summer sun, and its water bowl was empty. I ran in to the first floor and asked Marta why the animal, which had been so charming and had sat so close to her father, was now chained. She looked upon me as the ridiculous urbanite I seemed to her.

"The dog will be no good for truffle hunting if he is allowed to be a dog for company," she explained.

"But your father carried that dog around for months," I said.

"You give the dog affection so it understands that you are its master and it becomes attached to you," she said. "But then you must tie it up, or it becomes disobedient."

"It's not true," I said, but I couldn't compete with centuries of folk knowledge. I was a vegan hippie energy healer in Republican Alabama; nobody wanted to hear the touchy-feely nonsense I was spouting.

I sat for an hour next to the dog and brought it some water, but its fate was sealed.

These dogs scattered the countryside. Emanuele's Zio Gianni kept three anxious half-breeds in a dark, covered shed. They were allowed out a few times a year for hunting, but the rest of the time they just jumped up and down in their purgatory, barking at the top of their lungs.

"I know it's cruel," Gianni explained to me when I voiced my opinion, "but I haven't got time."

"Ma è una creatura," I pleaded. The word *creatura* implied a living being created by God, and God could get those Roman Catholics to do a whole lot.

"Look, life isn't fair. I work all day for the region, and they don't pay me enough," Gianni replied.

"Just because life isn't fair for you doesn't mean you should neglect them," I countered.

Gianni nodded; okay, I had a point. Soon he built the half-breeds a larger shed. They continued to peek through to daylight and jump up and down all day long, screeching, but they had a little more room. Once in a while, one was tied up just outside the shed, and as I approached, it growled and barked, but as soon as I came within touching distance, it threw itself into a sad, submissive posture, peed on the ground, and accepted affection with overwhelming gratitude.

THERE WAS THE FENCED PLOT in the back of the farm up the hill in which stood three hysterical dogs, each chained to its dilapidated doghouse by a short length of metal. One purebred hunting dog was relegated to the back, where it circled a dirt area and sat quietly all day, staring out. The other two—a sausage-shaped black and brown mongrel and a tall, wheat-colored hound mix—stood atop their shacks and barked from dawn to dusk. Once Marcus, still in heat, flew through the field by their cage, and the sausage-shaped dog lost his wits. He was barking and jumping in such a fury that he managed to thrust himself over a side of the fence that had sunken a bit. I looked up to see him hanging from his chain, which was connected to the doghouse.

I swore to myself as I ran to him. He had always seemed vicious, letting out furious yelps any time I passed. He was keeping himself from strangulation by precariously balancing his back paws in some of the fencing, but he didn't have long. He let out a roar as I got closer, but as soon as I was within arm's length, he grew quiet and docile. I grabbed his body, which stank, and pressed him to me, unable to detach him from the tangled chain. He did nothing to resist, and lay in my arms with some satisfaction. Finally, I ripped off his collar, and with that liberation, he pushed off me and sprinted into the field, where Marcus was jogging. He made a beeline for her and bit her firmly on the butt.

"Ingrate!" I screamed.

Soon, he was gone, and I was covered in brown sludge. The dog had been living in his own filth for years.

There was nothing more I could do for him, or for any of his contemporaries. Knowing no other option, he returned home even when he'd been given a chance at freedom. I saw him the next day. He was yelping uselessly, the chain once again fastened to his neck.

I EXAMINE THE FACES OF THE SLEEPING
DOGS BESIDE ME, THE IMPROBABLE
NATURE OF THEIR EXISTENCE, THE SHORT
LIVES THEY LIVE WITH AN INTENSITY
UNBEARABLE TO US.

—JIM HARRISON

LUIGI THE MINIATURE POODLE'S ELDERLY owner, who had
lent the pink collar to Marcus on her first day as my dog, was my
only kindred spirit. I bumped into her as we were both walking
down Via Todi one day. Marcus ran in circles around me, but Luigi
was tethered to a slender, rhinestone-studded leash. He had a perfect
gray bouffant cut, and his mistress tagged along behind him, wearing a long skirt and sweater, her white hair pressed into a bun.

She admired Marcus, asking how I'd come upon her. I told her
the story, and she looked pained. We passed a house where a yappy
blond terrier lived, and the old woman called him to her. She with-
drew a biscuit from her pocket and fed him, whispering, "Che dolce,
che cane dolce.

"The people around here cannot understand that the dog has
a soul, too," she said mournfully, before we parted. "They have
their reasons."

Indeed, the country mindset was not some random wrong-headedness, but a shared perspective born of generations of hardship. It didn't excuse their occasional cruelty, but it did explain it. When the people were starving, as they had been on and off for centuries, it hardly made sense to coddle puppies.

During World War II, when the already-impoverished townspeople tottered on the brink of mass starvation, grocer Gianfranco's grandfather, himself penniless, gave away food at no cost. For this, he was generally credited with saving the lives of dozens of local citizens. Mongrels congregated outside homes, begging for precious bits of bread that the children didn't even have. In an ancient country, sixty years wasn't much time: The Collelungese dog's main purpose was to hunt game that would sustain families. For that, it got kibble and a spot to lay its head. Old habits—especially old Italian habits—die hard.

I vecchi were of the last generation to suffer with no promise of reprieve. For Emanuele's grandparents, the only work available had been in other regions, in lumberyards or factories of Tuscany and the Marche, so all men of working age, with the exception of the priest and the grocer, were shipped off on six-month assignments to cut down the woods by hand. The women who stayed behind chopped firewood, harvested food, kept the livestock, and raised the children.

"But—what about sex?" I blurted out over dinner.

"What?" Serenella asked.

"Well, what did everyone do for sex?" I asked. "I mean, an entire town of women and just a few guys? And what did the men do all that time out in the woods?"

"Come to think of it," Fabio said, "I think the grocer and priest had a fantastic time!"

"We've been poor for a long time," said Emanuele.

Poverty led to particular tendencies. Fabio, for one, joined at least a third of the Collelungo population in his terror of dentists. This resulted in a good level of toothlessness, as the populace did not practice great dental hygiene and tended to smoke a lot. Renato tapped his shiny white dentures.

"Fake," he said cheerfully.

"Back in the 1960s, we didn't have a dentist," Fabio said.

"What if you had a toothache?"

"We walked to the old barbershop," he said. He pointed up the hill. "The barber was the only man in town willing to help with a bad tooth."

"What did the barber do?"

"He told you to sit down, and he took out some pliers," Fabio said. "And you saw the pliers and backed away, saying, 'You know, it's not so bad after all. . . . '"

Nonno Renato chuckled from his perch on the couch. "When I was in my twenties, I was so poor that the only shoes I could afford were one size too small. So I bought them, cut a hole for my big toe, and wore them for five years."

Most of the older folks had not been able to purchase cars until the mid-1980s, and while the women had never been taught to steer anything trickier than a wheelbarrow, the men had become accustomed to driving moped trucks made by the company Piaggio after the war. They were a sort of Vespa scooter with a tiny truck balanced on top: three-wheeled, open-backed vehicles with an uncomfortable cab for one in the front. The earliest models were steered by handlebars. Several vintage numbers could still be seen carting small loads around town.

Because of this, the older generation possessed a limited knowledge of driving and tended to put the car in first gear and go. No matter the landscape, they remained cheerfully in first gear. You could hear it coming from two miles off—the loud, metallic moan of the straining automobile attempting to transport them up a hill.

SO THEY HAD SOME *MOTIVI*, or reasons, for their behavior, but I still didn't want to put a litter of puppies in their midst. I circled Marcus every day, growing increasingly panicked as her belly further distended. Finally, I drove her to Dr. Massarelli. Was she with child?

"È possibile," he said slowly. He turned her on her side, shaved her belly, took out a tube of jelly, and smeared it across. Marcus lay very still, her legs stiffly outstretched, staring at me in horror. Dr. Massarelli pulled out a wand, which he ran along her underside. On the attached sonogram screen, I saw a mess of bowel and stomach, and peered in.

"Aha!" he said softly. He pointed at two black dots.

"Puppies?" I asked with alarm.

"Credo di sì," Dr. Massarelli said, looking very professorial. He studied the screen for a few more minutes. "Or maybe it is some food she is digesting."

When I returned to the Cruciani house, Serenella wanted to know the outcome.

"He looked in her stomach and said that either there were two puppies or two pieces of . . . poop," I said, sitting dejectedly on the couch. I was out twenty euros.

"So . . . either a puppy or a shit?" she asked, grinning. "Bravo dottore!"

In fact, it was *una cacca*. I never suspected that the day would come when excrement would make me happy. Marcus's stomach began to go down, though her nipples remained hard and her teats bloated for two months. She had experienced the hysterical pregnancy of which Fabio had warned, though not necessarily because she needed to satisfy her maternal urge. It was called canine false pregnancy and was common in female dogs, I found out by looking on the Internet at the grocery store. I read that certain bitches are sensitive to hormonal fluctuations and can present symptoms of pregnancy even when they're not pregnant. The symptoms—the distended belly, the full teats (some unfortunate creatures even lactated and appeared to go into labor)—would disappear in a month or so. Despite Ettore's plan to breed her, I would have Marcus secretly spayed so that this would never happen again.

MEANWHILE, MARCUS, RECOVERED FROM HER ordeal, had taken to living out her dream. Her dream was to kill a chicken. She began to devote a good deal of her day to standing motionless in a crouch outside the neighbor's chicken pen. She lowered herself to the ground like a tigress and slunk around the pen for hours. It occurred to me that she had probably spent the first year of her life sniffing those chickens from her confines across the orchard, plotting and planning.

Emanuele broke the news in spring. Marcus had been involved in a slaughter. She had killed three bunnies and six chickens that had wandered aimlessly out of a small hole in the coop. She had left their corpses strewn over the grounds and had briefly gone on the lam.

Like a parent blind to her child's faults, I initially denied the incident.

"She couldn't have," I squawked, even as I secretly recalled finding a mysterious spot of blood on Marcus's muzzle that morning—a spot of blood that could not be traced to a wound on her body. This was my meek and tender girl! I had once been a hard-nosed woman of reason, and now I was making unconvincing excuses for a dog that was clearly guilty of *pollo*cide. And, almost unspeakably, some of the victims had been bunnies—bunnies meant for the pot anyway, but bunnies nonetheless.

Emanuele insisted. The neighbor had witnessed the scene from his garden and had run down to stop it, but had been too late. We were just lucky that we didn't have to pay for the dead. Furthermore, Emanuele suggested that I consider caging Marcus again. If she continued to pillage the livestock, the farmer had a legal right to shoot her.

SO MARCUS HAD A TOUCH of savagery—we all had our faults, didn't we? And who could blame her; she was teeming with chicken-killing genes.

"Bunnies, Marcus?" I asked. She sat ramrod straight and searched my face for direction. "Nobody likes a bunny killer." Marcus cocked her head to the side and raised her ears. For her, the bunnies were probably an *amuse-bouche*.

Though it wasn't her fault, I needed to help her control her less appealing urges. After the false pregnancy and the murder spree, I decided that Marcus needed to change her life. She needed to live with us.

"I'd say you love that dog more than you love me," Emanuele observed, perhaps with a tinge of relief, and, defeated, he approved Marcus's move-in.

I placed a wicker bed on the floor and she hopped in, turned her body in a tight pretzel, and refused to move, except to eat some kibble and leave for a walk.

The neighbors peeked from their windows, gasping as the brute emerged from a dwelling made only for immaculate humans. I had created a great scandal.

"Giustina, mi fa schifo," Serenella said. It grosses me out.

"Un cane in casa?" Nonna Ferrina murmured. "Ma no . . . no . . . no!" Nonna Ferrina usually let out a little scream of fear whenever the dog was nearby, which in turn frightened Marcus, so that eventually, when they saw each other, each balked.

When Marcus had been in my house for several weeks, I made her an appointment to be spayed. Dr. Massarelli shaved a patch of fur on her slender front leg and inserted a needle. In a minute, Marcus had slipped into blissful oblivion, her tense body softening and then slumping as I lowered her to the table.

When I arrived to pick her up in the afternoon, she was hardly awake, and the vet was sweating from the forehead.

"Could you give me a hand for a moment?" he asked.

He ushered me into the operating room, where a tiny female dog with long, speckled fur and large, batlike ears was lying, her eyes glazed over, her breath deep and uneven. Her abdomen was stitched up with black thread. Nearby, in a basket, a pair of just-born pups was mewling beneath a heat lamp. As the doctor explained it, the pups must have had a large father, as they were too big for a natural birth, and the mother, in distress, had been brought in for a Caesarean. I bent down to the basket. The pups' eyes were closed, and they were moving their toothless mouths and emitting little cries. If the mother did not wake up and feed them, the veterinarian said, the pups were goners. He gave me gloves and told me to massage them while the mother came to. I sat on the floor beneath the harsh surgical lights and moved my hand over their warm, new bodies. They were the size of hamsters, completely unprepared to go it on their own, hoping for milk, needing touch in order to survive.

When the vet's assistant returned, he took over the pups and I collected Marcus, whose shaved pink underside had been cut open and sewn together, and carried her to the car. Then I carried her to the house and made a bed for her on the couch, where she went to sleep. For a moment, I regretted putting her through what looked like such a brutal process, and I reflected on the Italians' protestations. I had the disconcerting sensation that I had chosen for her something that went against nature, but I put that out of my head.

When Marcus awoke, she was in pain, and she fixed me with

her liquid eyes, as though perhaps I could explain the hurt to her, or I could do something to help. I sat next to her, feeling her stare, and finally turned to her. I had never picked her up before, but I pushed my arms under her and moved her around so that she was lying on my lap like a small person, cradled in my arms. I covered her with a blanket, and she laid her head against my chest and fell fast asleep.

I had been an avid comic-book collector as a child and had even racked up an impressive three thousand assorted issues of *Archie*. In one of the Marvels I sometimes picked up, a superhero saved another's life and then sighed, irritated that he was now forever responsible for the person he'd rescued. After swooping a girl up from train tracks or out of a burning car, this annoyed (and smitten) superhero followed her around, keeping a constant vigil as she went about her daily routine. It had struck me as such a perplexing deal that I remembered it almost twenty years after reading it: Why, once you did one pretty significant favor for someone, would you then be committed to keeping her safe forever on? The superhero's initial train-track feat, I thought, should be enough; he should be able to move on guiltlessly, to devote his time to other hobbies. As Marcus slept on my lap, I finally understood the deal: I had willfully shifted another being's course, and that meant that I was technically morally bound to ensure her well-being for a lifetime.

IT ALL SEEMS STUPID NOW,
BUT WAS NATURAL THEN.

—M. F. K. FISHER

POP QUIZ: WHAT IS THE healthy, rational approach to the knowledge that you are involved in a dead-end relationship in a foreign country? Do you book a ticket home? Take a language class to make the most of your remaining time? Devote your emotional energy to analyzing why your relationship is tanking?

Or do you become hopelessly enmeshed with a scrawny dog and then, suddenly, impulsively buy, *with* your unfit significant other (that's right: as a joint endeavor!), an untamed horse? And then, after that purchase, do you acquire, using the last of your savings, another untamed horse, resulting in the shared (shared with your clearly incongruous, unsuitable significant other, that is) ownership of a total of two wild horses? Perhaps the next step is to locate the youngest, most unstable female trainer in the country (possibly even the continent)? Maybe find her a hovel down the street, allowing her excellent access to the underbelly of your already-fragile affair?

Choose to go out with a bloody bang, not one of those boring, sensible, relatively painless whimpers?

Though I saw the winding down of the love between Emanuele and me, I did not book a ticket home, sign up for Italian lessons, or analyze the wheres, whys, and hows of our failing affair. My behavior calls to mind that of a formerly buttoned-down CEO who was arrested a few years back. He had embarked on a raucous bender during which he blew through company savings, snorted piles of fine cocaine, and enjoyed the services of a particularly limber prostitute. When the authorities interviewed him at his arraignment, they asked him why he had done what he had done. He looked at them, his face contorted with profound confusion, and said, "Well, I guess I just went a little crazy."

EMANUELE AND I HAD BEEN following the World Dart Championships on ESPN. Pasty Brits who appeared to have spent their lives in murky bars, never eating anything greener than a plate of peas mashed with mayonnaise, demonstrated mechanical accuracy and skill. Winter's boredom had driven us to such depths, and we convinced ourselves that we were purchasing a horse to give us another activity as soon as the weather broke. We also liked to pretend that we wanted to purchase the horse as a way for me to entertain myself; Emanuele had scored the nonspeaking role of a drunken scamp in a local production of a Chekhov play, and he would be gone often, rehearsing. I went to the play in the spring and watched as he lolled about silently, dressed in rags, for two hours. If he could take up theater as a hobby, I could get a horse.

In the early spring, Emanuele and I purchased a young half-breed Appaloosa from his cousin Flavio. I had first seen her within the fenced field below Flavio's house. He had raised her without training her, but he no longer had the desire or ability to care for two horses (he had long owned a pouty Irish draft mix that I eventually convinced him to name Emma).

The filly was delicate, at two years of age not quite finished growing. She was light brown, speckled with white, and ran to me to eat grass from my hand, brushing her heavy lips across my palm. She cost five hundred euros. Since the Appaloosa was originally a Native American breed, I named her Tallulah, which, according to the Internet, meant "leaping water" in Choctaw. I had presented a series of names to the Crucianis, reading from a notebook at their kitchen table. Tallulah was most pleasing to the Italian ear.

"It means, you know, water that jumps," I tried to explain in my limited Italian, and they smiled benevolently.

"Carina," Serenella offered. Pretty.

Daisy, Ettore's white mare, awaited Tallulah down at the Cruciani house. Daisy had always seemed to be a very ordinary horse with the ability to gallop at remarkable speeds. She was Ettore's unfortunate ward, which I later learned accounted for what I first understood as grumpiness but soon came to see was a fundamental distrust of people. On that day, Daisy was in heat, and visibly annoyed.

I cleared out a space for Tallulah near her new stall, which Ettore and Emanuele had banged together in a day. I pushed the stiff broom across the floor. I painted name signs for the horses, Daisy and Tallulah, black on white, and filled Tallulah's stall with hay that Emanuele had cut, rolled, and dried as I bopped around with him on a rusty tractor. I placed a bucket of water in the corner.

I had ridden horses when I was younger, but it had never occurred to me that they did not simply spring up in the stable, fully able to turn right when the bit pushed their mouth, so when I managed to put the harness around Tallulah's muzzle and lead her out onto the street, I was struck by her strength and unpredictability. She was anxious and powerful. If she knew her force, or used it, I would be a sad match.

Emanuele drove along by my side, with Marcus peering out tentatively from the passenger seat, looking thrilled to be acquiring a horse of her own. We turned right onto Via Todi and clopped along, past the bar and its elderly audience, and down to the Cruciani residence. When I had removed Tallulah from the pasture, the Irish draft horse had begun to wail at the separation, and we could still hear mournful baying in the distance.

Meanwhile, Ettore stood in front of Casa Cruciani in his ripped T-shirt and his cowboy hat, smoking a stub of a heavy cigarette, talking on his cell phone, and holding a chain that connected to Daisy's worn leather halter. When the two horses saw each other—Tallulah poised halfway down the hill and Daisy twenty yards away in the driveway—they simultaneously came unglued, baying and bucking. Ettore and I clung to their ropes and chains, each of us trying to appear at least a little bit calm. Daisy promptly emptied her bowels and then dragged a barely contained Ettore over to Tallulah, where she turned around and placed her behind in Tallulah's face. Her enlarged vagina emitted a white substance. Her nostrils expanded.

"Sono innamorate," Ettore remarked.

"Lesbiche?" I asked.

"Eh, beh . . . perché no?" Fabio said.

With the promise of food, we had convinced Tallulah to enter her stall. She scratched her head against the wooden slats and stood facing the back corner, and then she eliminated straight into her water bucket.

Marcus ate some of the oats scattered on the ground and then perched on a bale of hay, straining her neck to check on the horses, whom she seemed to regard with immense respect. Tallulah kicked the door and Daisy roared from across the garage, infuriated by the distance between them. I stood, awed by Tallulah in her stall. I wished to take a ride, but she wasn't ready to accept the saddle. We called Lucia, a minor legend in these parts.

＊

LUCIA: SEMIPROFESSIONAL LOCAL HORSE-TAMER. SHE
was twenty-one years old, with a tangled mop of jet black hair, cold
blue eyes against sun-scorched skin, the face of a child, and the
cracked hands of an ancient farmer. Lucia lived on a grand, isolated,
mostly defunct farm twenty minutes from any paved road. From
afar, the estate looked as if it was cradled in a meteor crater—a flat
round space in the middle of so much hill country. Dying vines,
cramped from dehydration and neglect, their grapes shriveled and
dusty, lined the first half of the long, winding driveway and then
gave way to twisted olive groves, and soon a rambling stone house. A
German shepherd bitch with milky white eyes sat listlessly by the
front door in all but the coldest weather. The dirt zone around the
house was covered in watering cans and broken flowerpots. A gaggle
of geese meandered about the earth, screeching at anything that
came too close, and a long-haired, slate gray cat eyed visitors from the
hood of a white Volvo sedan sitting on cinder blocks.

Lucia lived with her yellow-haired Dutch mother, who was red
faced and heavyset, and her fourteen-year-old sister, who was slight,
proper, and blonde. Three months before we met, Lucia's salesman
father had died alone of a heart attack in a corporate hotel in Ger-
many, and the house itself seemed paused in a state of grief. The first
floor was one vast and dusty room with only a few scattered square
windows. On the hottest day of August, it was cold and dark in that
room, and the spartan furnishings made it feel cavernous. A pair of
show-quality border collies lived there. The kitchen housed the cages
of eight exotic birds and an aquarium where colorful fish swam. A
glossy chestnut quarter horse pranced in an immaculately tended,
fenced backyard.

Lucia emerged from her house as though she were escaping
from prison, her feet soft on the ground. She was in control of her

body, which had the musculature of a professional athlete: sturdy, with broad, defined shoulders, distinct biceps, small breasts, and a tight waist. Her backside was unavoidable: firm and hard as an apple, sitting high.

"I'm entranced by her ass," I once whispered to Ettore as she worked with a horse.

"Tell me about it," he whispered back.

She slid into the back of our car in her dark brown leather cowboy boots and blue jeans.

"Piacere," she said softly, flashing her bashful, lopsided smile. The corner of one of her front teeth was chipped. She reached forward and clutched my hand firmly. Her nails had been bitten to the nub, and her hands were raw. She pulled a Lucky Strike from the package she kept clenched in her left fist and lit it. Then she leaned back into the seat and exhaled.

Once in Collelungo, Lucia led Tallulah down through Fabio's olive grove, which ran the length of a tall hill, and into a flat, wooded area below. Emanuele and I sat on a fallen log a distance away, and Marcus left us to explore the area. From the outside, Umbrian forests are an expanse of thick, unyielding green. Where no towns are carved from this expanse, where no fields are plowed, the dense forest offers no relief. The forest is dark beneath the crowded trees. The interior woods are a labyrinth of tree trunks, dusty rocks, dry fallen leaves, water trickling down a stream.

Lucia found a space in which she and the horse could stand comfortably, where there were not too many trees in the way. She threw her cigarette butt on the ground, stomped it with the heel of her boot, and tightened her hold on Tallulah. For a moment, she stood, facing the horse. Then, she gathered up the slack rope, whipped one end around, and slapped Tallulah on the rump with it. Tallulah began to flee, but Lucia pulled her back and repeated the exercise: slap, flee, return. She and Tallulah entered into a dance: Lucia stepped in,

Tallulah stepped back, Lucia hit Tallulah's rump, Tallulah ran. After twenty minutes of such struggle, Tallulah began to trot around Lucia, creating a circle, pulling taut the rope. At one point, Lucia walked in toward the horse and pressed her forehead against Tallulah's, and they both let out a deep sigh.

"She understands," Lucia said, pulling back. This strange exercise had communicated to the horse that Lucia would be the leader. Lucia pulled the crushed box of Lucky Strikes from her pocket. She wiped her forehead, leaving a thin layer of dirt behind. Then she moved closer to Tallulah and began to massage the animal's long neck, now damp with sweat.

Tallulah was a relatively easy horse to train. *Intelligente.* Day after day, Emanuele and I drove to Lucia's doleful farm. She was usually late getting in the car and would often disappear into the house for fifteen minutes, trying to find a shoe or a lighter. Sometimes, her arm or cheek was marked with a burn or a bruise. Her mother, she confessed, came at her, and the two of them fought, hurling dishes and punching each other as the little sister looked on. But since Lucia had no money and no car, she eventually retreated into polite tones. When she spoke to her mother on the telephone, her voice turned childlike and small, and she agreed to all demands made of her, saying again and again, "Sì, Mamma. Grazie, Mamma." Sometimes we picked Lucia up at her job in a restaurant off a stretch of asphalt on the way to Todi. Lucia was the dishwasher. Her mother took her money, she said, for room and board.

With Tallulah, Lucia was firm and in command, but also sweet. Tallulah balked the first time she wore a saddle, kicking up dust and stomping her hooves. Lucia mounted the furious horse in the middle of the pasture, and as Tallulah began to buck, Lucia held on. If she allowed herself to be thrown off, she would teach the horse that by bucking, it could accomplish its goal; otherwise, bucking was exhausting for a horse, and if it served no purpose, the horse would give up on it. So she sat in the saddle like a piece of iron—her legs, all their strength, pressed down on the stirrups, and as Tallulah rose up, Lucia rose, too, unresisting. She and Tallulah melded, so that the motion was singular—one being tossing itself up and down. In the end, when Tallulah surrendered, they were both soaked in sweat, Tallulah's shoulder and quarters foaming. Lucia had never wavered, and she sat triumphantly atop the horse.

IN MY BOUT OF INSANITY, I decided that Tallulah was not sufficient: Emanuele and I needed another horse. This horse would be my horse, not our horse. Lucia had offered to train the horse for free, which made it a good investment, because any horse would rise in value when it had been professionally shaped up.

"Be careful when you take her," Ettore said to Emanuele and Lucia, pointing at me. "These farms don't treat the beasts gently."

Gianni the horse vendor wasn't around on that day.

"He went to Perugia to eat fish," a wizened farmhand with four teeth explained. The same farmhand, who weighed less than I, later wandered past me, smiled widely, and vigorously slapped my derriere.

Instead, Gianni's teenage son showed us a small barn in which a lovely thoroughbred was well kept. There were several miniature ponies—no more than three feet high—cramped in their own stalls, and the boy coaxed one out and rode it for us, hitting it with a crop as it struggled to support his weight. The boy was larger than the miniature horse, and his legs were long enough that he merely stepped over its back, and when he rode, he had to hold his feet up above the ground.

The horses were kept in three separate paddocks. In one paddock, protected by an electric fence, lived a handsome family of pure Sicilian horses: a stallion, his mare, two daughters, and a son. They were sleek, mahogany colored, and tall. A white patch of hair in the shape of a star grew on each of their foreheads. They were not for sale.

In the bottom two paddocks, Gianni held a group of horses, most of which could be purchased for under five hundred euros. They were old horses, just a step away from being sent off to the equine meat factory, and they ambled around the chalky land, longing for a mouthful of grass growing from soil that had long ago been picked clean. In the middle of the paddocks, Gianni placed a round of hay, but the horses were rarely given oats.

There was nothing for us there; Lucia refused to give business to someone whose horses were so thin and mangy.

The next horse vendor we visited was Ovidio, who lived on the edge of another highway off the gleaming historic city of Orvieto, on a huge plot of untamed land nestled in between factories and warehouses. When we arrived at Ovidio's house, his daughter—a young teenager with curly hair and braces—leaned out from the second-floor window of their villa.

"Mio padre arriva subito," she said, flashing us a metallic smile.

We walked around the house. In a small wooden cell stood a spectacular caramel-colored horse. Nearby, there was a barn broken up into sections. The first section seemed to be a makeshift lodging for a laborer: a large, unkempt cot with a T-shirt crumpled up on the navy duvet, a bottle of cheap vodka, an empty water container, some worn shirts hanging from hooks, and an overflowing ashtray. The rest of the room was left just as it would have been for an animal: cement floors and walls, bits of hay scattered about.

The next section was a feed room, and the final section was a chasmal space that looked like an abandoned milking room. Through the long area ran a metal bar separating one side from the next. A family of tiny goats stood in a gated rectangle at the edge of the room—a mother and her kids. The kids were no bigger than adult cats, and they clamored for milk. Lucia hopped over the gate and into their space. To the mother goat's chagrin, Lucia scooped up one of the babies and held it to her.

"Che bello!" she exclaimed. "Che dolce!"

Then she handed it over to me. The little animal weighed no more than twenty pounds. It whined and looked at its distraught mother. Its hooves, not yet developed, were soft to the touch, and it had a set of small, square teeth that looked human. The baby was warm, and it smelled like hay. I put it back with its mother, and we returned to the front of the house, sat at a picnic table near a roaming German shepherd, and waited.

Twenty minutes had passed when we saw a commotion in the distance. There was an underpass beneath the far-off highway, and somebody was coming through. Walking closer, I saw a strange scene. A white-haired man slowly drove a worn-out Jeep over the land. In front of him, a slouchy Romanian worker grappled with an enraged black stallion. The stallion was tall and muscular, and it had no intention of being coaxed anywhere. It pulled backward, forward, and sideways and let out cries of terror and fury. The worker—sweat-slicked, wearing only a pair of ripped old leather loafers on his feet, despite the heavy hooves landing just inches from them—was at the mercy of the stallion. The man never uttered a sound, but he carried an expression of despair, his face dull but his eyes alive with fear as he silently jerked back and forth. When they neared the house, Ovidio lowered himself from the Jeep. He walked with a limp; one of his hips fell three inches below the other.

Ovidio had known Lucia for years. First, he had seen her in the cutting circuit, a sport in which a rider is judged on her ability to separate a cow from the herd. She had been riding since the age of seven, when she was given a miniature horse. For a while, she had ridden in the English style, sitting on the smooth saddle, feet in high stirrups, posting as she trotted. But English style was too restrained for her tastes, and she soon found that she liked the challenge of stallions—her favorite was a locally famous quarter horse aptly named Tabasco—and the gallop. She had switched to riding western style—or American style, as the Italians called it.

Since then, Lucia had become a champion at cutting. There were few Texan-style cattle farms in Italy, so the competition was purely a contest of control: How quickly could you stop and turn your horse, to mimic blocking the sharp zigzag of a cow trying to rejoin its herd? Later, when she had apprenticed under a maestro of horse training ("training twenty horses a day sometimes"), she had bought and sold horses, and some had come from or gone to Ovidio.

Ovidio greeted her with a kiss and excused himself to return to his task: forcing the stallion into the barn. He limped over to the animal and began to hit it with a slim stick. As he beat the animal from behind, the Romanian pulled it forward. The Romanian stood halfway inside the barn, poised at a forty-five-degree angle, all his weight bearing down on the rope, and Ovidio stood on the grass, slamming the stick against the stallion. The stallion became increasingly agitated, and when it had been forced to the door frame, it threw itself toward the brick, hitting its head loudly first on the side and then on the top: bone against stone. I looked at Lucia and Emanuele, feeling suddenly ill.

"I have an idea," Lucia interrupted, stepping up to Ovidio. "May I?" Gratefully, the Romanian backed away, and Ovidio handed Lucia the rope.

Lucia moved in close to the stallion and placed a hand over his left eye. He closed his eye, and she began to massage the eyeball and the surrounding area. Then she moved directly in front of him and massaged both eyes. The stallion stopped resisting, relaxing his fine body. Lucia requested a cut of rope, which Ovidio brought to her. She tied a length of it to the stallion's front leg and began, slowly, to pull him in—first one halting step, then another. Ovidio stood behind with his stick, and just as the stallion took another step in, he smacked him, and the stallion flew backward. Lucia stood up, hiding her exasperation. They would try again, and again, until finally the stallion walked into the barn, where he was tied to a post and left to wait for the farrier, and then a buyer.

After this ordeal, Ovidio invited us into his house, up the staircase to the dim second-floor room, where his wife, a quiet woman with her hair in a twist, served us glasses of syrupy fruit punch. He asked Lucia about her father's death, and Lucia began to cry as she detailed the somber, fishy tale of his lonely passing. I sipped my fruit punch and gazed at the imposing oil portrait of a man in military dress. The place felt like an abandoned fortress: Every surface seemed to be constructed of charcoal-colored stone.

After offering grave condolences to Lucia, Ovidio took us down to view his wares: several heavy yellow geldings, a tall German jumping mare that required expertise, a jet black filly with a white star on her forehead. Lucia would test each of them. On one round, she fought a caramel-colored Hanover, pulling on her reins to no avail as the Hanover sped hysterically around the ring. After a battle for the title of *capo,* or boss—Lucia would never let a horse dominate her, and used all her might and skill to convince the animal to do what she wanted—she dismounted and led the glistening Hanover back to us. She shot me a stern look.

"This is *not* the horse for you," she said stonily.

Lucia rode them all, trotting and galloping and walking around the jumping ring. I watched from a far side of the ring, near a pair of gloomy donkeys drinking from a dirty trough under the main road that rose above Ovidio's farm. Ultimately, no matter how beautiful the horse, Lucia refused. She seemed to see what we could not: a bad knee, an awkward trot, antisocial behavior with other horses. One horse, a puny, knock-kneed gelding named Vulcan, was presented to us like a racing thoroughbred to a queen. Ovidio, it turned out, was desperate to get it off his hands.

"Ovidio asked me to convince you two to buy Vulcan," Lucia said from her perch in the backseat as we drove off the farm. "He said he'd give me 25 percent if I told you to buy that one for eight hundred euros, but the horse was worth no more than fifty euros."

"The horse vendor is not the most honorable of men," Emanuele said.

"Can't we find a better vendor?" I asked.

"No," they both said at once. For our money, there wasn't one.

⟋⟍

WE TRAVERSED THE COUNTRYSIDE FOR weeks, Lucia in the backseat, Emanuele driving, and Marcus and I squeezed together up front. Until we found our horse, we could not rest.

Emanuele and I were like the doctor who keeps pressing down on the patient's chest even after he has died, hysterically screaming, "*Live, live, live, damn it!*" Or the warring couple that gets pregnant in order to stay together: fueled by hope and denial, committed to a task that is futile at best and destructive at worst.

There are hundreds of reasons that explain why otherwise sane human beings try so vigorously to repair romantic relationships that are clearly forever broken: We are afraid of failure, of loneliness, of abandonment, of the future, of change. We hate to admit that we've made a mistake, that we've wasted time, money, our love. We hang back, terrified, and refuse to step into the next unknown realm.

I don't know why Emanuele hoped to maintain it—surely there was nothing left for him to gain. He no longer whispered, "I love you and I want you to love so much me," or, "I love you, amore, but I don't have such a great dictionary to tell you with three hundred thousand words how much I love you." But still, in his vague and uncommitted way, he cared for me. He may have been late to every engagement we ever had, and he may have neglected me, but on my birthday, he bought me a small, pretty diamond ring, and for Valentine's Day, he had an awkward-looking woman from a nearby village knock on the door while he was at work and hand me three red roses bound in a complicated wooden travel vase. San Valentino was rumored to come from Terni. We went to the annual fair, and Emanuele ordered a key chain for me, engraved on the spot with the Bob Dylan lyric from "Abandoned Love." *Justine,* my silver key chain said, *I love you but you're strange.*

"In English because she is American," Emanuele said.

"Ahh, sei americana?" asked the engraver. "Democrat or Republican?"

Likely, Emanuele felt a sense of responsibility for my happiness, as I had given up my home to enter his. Even if he did not have the capacity to satisfy my needs, he did try, in his own way. In his defense, I was the Justine of the engraved key chain: possibly lovable, but definitely (especially to an Italian gardener) strange.

Or perhaps Emanuele went ahead with buying the horse because he was simply afraid of being alone again. He never explained his motivation, because when I had the chance to ask, I didn't know how to. He probably wouldn't have been able to give me an answer anyway.

For me, the quest for horses was my final stand of resistance. It was the result of an internal war that pitted my intuition against my perceived need. My intuition told me to leave, but my perceived need—stronger, more determined—fought for me to stay, to nest. Screw common sense and my own instincts: I wanted me some wild horses!

Sometimes when I thought of leaving, I counteracted it with a fantasy. I imagined Marcus and my horse and me gliding over the hills. This way, Emanuele could have his friends and his familial circle and I could have mine, though mine would be composed of, apparently, a dog and a horse or two. The flawed logic was, basically, that if Marcus made me happy, a fabulous horse could only make me happier. And this way, I would not have to return to New York City and a life and persona that no longer fit; I could fix my broken relationship and hide forever in the burnt-amber hills of Collelungo.

Also, I was being impatient, which may be the reason most people settle down. *Enough,* we say weakly. Enough with making eyes, with picking one from the multitudes, with praying that he or she picks you back. Enough with the introductions, the little dance of acceptance or rejection, the nervous banter, the extra glass (or three) of wine, the obsessive wish for the phone call, the first triumphant kiss. Enough with the negotiations and compromises; the initial excitement fading into familiarity, the thump of disappointment. And then you're expected to do it all over again?

$$\sim$$

EVERY DAY, WE DEVOTEDLY COLLECTED Lucia. After her work washing dishes, she began to walk in the direction of Collelungo, so I often came upon her on the side of the road. She walked forcefully, her short hair tangled, carrying nothing; she looked like a young boy from afar, with her cocky stride and her straight, strong figure. When she wore makeup, if she went out after dark, it looked as if she had drawn it on shakily with a crayon—two thick, uneven black lines surrounding her eyes. Once at the pub, having been insulted, she flew toward another girl, swinging her arms and puffing her nostrils like a little bull, only to be pulled back by three men and ordered to walk around on the outdoor patio to calm down.

"Che stronza, che figlia di puttana!" she muttered. What an bitch, what a daughter of a whore!

She was not exactly a proper lady, but you couldn't call her boring, which, it was becoming abundantly clear, was my single requirement for allowing someone complete access to my life. When we passed cyclists on the winding Umbrian roads, Lucia taunted them for kicks.

"Hey! Can't you go any faster, you asshole?" she hollered as we zipped by some spandex-clad athlete, pedaling with all his might. For several weeks, she held her cheek tight, moaning about a wisdom tooth. When she finally made an appointment with the dentist, she canceled it a day beforehand.

"I have decided that if I have respect for how all my animals are made, why can't I have respect for me?" she said. "I'm keeping my bad tooth."

Soon enough, we were eating dinner with Lucia almost every night. She cleaned the dishes and then climbed onto the couch next to me, smoking her heavy cigarettes and asking for advice on her skin, which was usually covered in a light spray of acne, and on her mother, who had once again taken her paycheck.

Lucia had run away from home a year earlier, she told me, and because of this, her mother had given her horse to her little sister. The horse—the one kept in a pen near the family farm—was worth twenty-five thousand euros, according to Lucia, who had trained it by herself. It was an impressive four-year-old quarter horse, worthy of showing, but Lucia was no longer permitted to go near it, and her voice cracked when she told me this. Her mother had insisted that she take the job washing dishes to pay for her food. Her forays with us were her only interaction with horses, and she felt that they were keeping her sane.

"Mi sento sola," she said. Alone. Sometimes she leaned up against me and cried for Pappa.

So: Lucia felt *sola,* about which I knew just a little bit. She loved the creatures, as did I. She even said, "I bet you wish Marcus was so small that you could fit her in your pocket," and she was right! I wished Marcus were entirely portable about seven times a day! How did she know? Therefore, while another, savvier individual with a different background might have watched her engage in fisticuffs during an otherwise pleasant night of Italian folk karaoke and thought, "Bad news," I thought, "A project!"

So, every afternoon before dusk, Lucia stood in the field, with a small audience of locals gathered beneath the olive trees, and shaped Tallulah, pushing and pulling, moving her mouth with the halter and then, slowly, the bit. Tallulah became more trustworthy, capable of adjusting her speed according to her rider's orders, unlikely to buck, seeming to understand what was being communicated to her. The Collelungese began to call Lucia *dottoressa*.

"They show me much tenderness here," Lucia said. With our help, she was finding her place. Lucky for her, I thought, peeling off a tentacle of jealousy.

WE DROVE TO A LAKE town near Terni. This particular lake town looked like some ruined Riviera—bleak and uninhabited, but with grand infrastructure. The promenade by the lake was scattered in trash, and a few damp restaurants sat empty, looking out upon the still, gray water. Some tourists bought fried treats from a window, and Marcus refused to get out of the car, huddling on the floor. We had found an ad in the newspaper: six-year-old quarter horse, two thousand euros. Emanuele cleaned out his savings, and we went to meet the owner.

The owner of the quarter horse was an old man whose brilliant white hair stood on end as though he kept his finger permanently stuck in a socket. His face was deep with lines, and his dull clothes hung off his thin frame. He had an unusually deep, throaty voice and barked out, when we met him at the foot of a highway underpass in an industrial center, that we were ten minutes late, and he wouldn't stand for that nonsense. We followed him from the industrial center through some untamed rural mountain roads and up a steep incline to a flat, fenced area, where a thick, chocolate-colored quarter horse kicked up dust from the ground. Lucia nodded at me enthusiastically.

"È splendido," she whispered. It was true: The horse was a strong and splendid specimen, standing in its dusty pen. It was nothing like the mutts that belonged to the highway-side vendors. This was a horse with some lineage, with an air of nobility.

The nameless quarter horse trotted over to us and offered its muzzle, sniffing each of us. Marcus, discombobulated by the long drive and overwhelmed with curiosity, crept beneath the fence and sidled up to the horse. Slowly, the horse bent its neck to the ground, staring Marcus in the eyes. Marcus crouched low, paralyzed, and shot me a regretful sidelong glance; she should never have entered this horse's lair. The horse stomped one foot.

"She wants to play," Lucia said. But Marcus didn't care about the horse's wishes; she backed away and then scampered to safety behind my legs.

Lucia rode the horse around its area, nodding at us: It had a smooth, calm gait. The man loved this horse, he said, but no longer could care for it. It had not been ridden in two years, but for Lucia, it trotted smoothly along. She was sold. She was a sucker for quarter horses, and this was a lovely example of the breed: good-natured, intelligent, graceful.

Now, while we were deciding, the old man wondered if we would like to see his other animals.

"Of course," we all said in unison, hoping only to befriend him and thus wrangle a lower price for the horse.

The old man slid into the passenger seat of our two-door car, so Marcus and I moved back with Lucia. Marcus struggled beneath my legs, and the skin of my bare arm stuck to the skin of Lucia's arm. Cigarette smoke billowed into the windowless backseat as both the man and Emanuele lit cigarettes, and the man directed Emanuele down the road. After several minutes on a paved street, we hit farmland and headed up into the low hills until the old man directed Emanuele to stop.

First, there was the goat and the donkey, he announced proudly. We got out of the car and approached a pen. There, we admired an enormously fat goat and an enormously fat donkey leaning against each other in a large grazing paddock surrounded by razor wire.

"They're the finest of friends," the man said.

"They're very beautiful," Lucia said with a bit too much enthusiasm.

We drove further, to a suburban tract of houses. On the side lawn of one of the identical houses stood an enormously fat white horse, connected by a chain to a stake in the ground.

"It's marvelous, no?" the old man asked, pacing around the animal.

"È fantastico," I said unconvincingly. The horse was very short.

"Just out of curiosity, what do you feed your horse?" Lucia asked.

"Loaves and loaves of bread," the man answered proudly. "It keeps them round."

We continued on to a field hidden by brush off the side of the road. We made our way through the bushes and came upon an enormously fat gray mother horse grazing next to her enormously fat baby.

"Attenta il cane," the man said to me, looking at Marcus. "A while back, a wolf dog came by here, trying to joke with the little baby. The mother kicked him once, with her back leg, and that wolf dog was dead, just like that." I quickly returned to the car and closed Marcus inside. For about ten minutes, we gamely admired the fat gray mother and fat gray baby.

We returned to the quarter horse. I held out my hand. It trotted over and began to lick me with its heavy tongue. Sure, it was
pudgy, what with the bread it had been eating, but it was ultimately
a prime creature, so glossy and muscled, and *dolce* enough to lick my
hand. After so many horses, so many miles covered, this was the first
horse that seemed to be a contender. Lucia promised that she could
be ridden soon, perhaps after a bit of fine-tuning. When we were
finally back in the car, we decided that this was the horse for us.
That night, I could hardly sleep. I could suddenly relate to all the
little girls around the world who dreamed of their very own pony.

MY HORSE, HOWEVER, WAS NO pony.

The day of her arrival, we traveled back to the lakeside town
and met the old man at a storage facility near a barren field off a
smoggy thoroughfare. The man's storage facility contained a large
truck made of thin, dented metal. We would load the horse, and
then the old man would follow us to Collelungo.

The horse had other ideas. Already agitated, she was unwilling
to enter the truck. Lucia was at work, so for an hour, Emanuele
coaxed the horse, as I stood a yard away, looking on as the frightened
animal resisted entrance, throwing her body about, neighing and
snorting, and then, finally, relenting. When the horse entered the
trailer, it turned back and caught my gaze, and for a minute, I had
my doubts. The man and Emanuele tied the horse to the sides of the
truck and closed it. She stomped on the metal; she would have to
brace herself for the journey, sliding on the slippery floor.

"And now, I need the girl with me," the man said. He could not
legally transport a horse in his truck. If he were pulled over, he reasoned, perhaps the presence of a young American would convince
the *polizia* that we were ignorant rather than purposefully unlawful.
I hopped up onto the worn seat, and we took off, the wild-eyed horse

whinnying in the back, Emanuele speeding ahead, avoiding the highways.

The man wore a tank top, and his arms were brown and gnarled. He liked to talk, and so we chatted about life and family, Italy and America, his former career as a businessman, his perverse passion for his pudgy animals; he was an enthusiastic conversationalist, and I enjoyed using my Italian. Every twenty minutes, I peered anxiously through a slat at the horse, which was sweating profusely, covered in white lather, and breathing heavily.

"Are you sure she's all right?" I asked, and the old man nodded confidently.

With every curve, she had to steel herself to avoid falling, and I could hear a chorus of banging and clanging.

To distract myself, I found more topics of discussion. The man and I spoke of travel and of my desire to cover the globe. He had no such desire; his home was the only place he wanted to be. Then I mentioned that I had spent several months in Tanzania.

"In *Africa?*" the man asked, shaking his head. "I would never go to Africa."

"Why not?" I asked.

"Black people carry venereal disease," he said casually.

I looked at him for a few seconds. His hands were on the wheel, one foot on the gas, one on the brake. We passed a sunflower field, bursting with *girasoli,* huge and yellow, balanced on heavy green stalks. Emanuele had driven far ahead, and now we were only guessing that he had traveled the road we were currently on.

"You believe that all black people carry venereal disease?" I asked.

"Ma, certo!" he said. "If I see a black person in a bar, I walk away. I don't want to get infected."

"You believe you can be infected by venereal disease by standing in the same space as a black person?" I asked.

"Certo!" he said with a look of conviction. "I don't take chances with stuff like that. Do you think I'm *matto*?"

"Era proprio matto lui!" I later said to a *vecchio,* describing the man's views. But the local looked at me strangely and remained silent, and I could not understand if he was having trouble with my Italian or if, on some level, he agreed with the man. After all, I had recently discovered that some older locals of a particular political persuasion still displayed in their homes—illegally, but without incident—portraits of Mussolini.

When we arrived in Collelungo, the neighborhood's young men were waiting for the horse. For these men, a horse was a status symbol, like a car or a motorcycle, and they were immediately impressed and overwhelmed with jealousy.

"Che bel cavallo," the men exclaimed, as the new quarter horse stood, steaming, on the grass, bending down to eat some herbs from the ground. I held her tenuously, the rope slack, and then she pulled me to and fro, moving toward a more luscious patch of grass. I had secret dreams for this horse. She would accept me as her leader, accept my hand on her soft muzzle, and we would ride through the countryside with Marcus close behind, needing only each other.

At one point, when the men had departed, Fabio passed by, walking down from the woodpile.

"Isn't she wonderful?" I asked, still holding the horse's rope.

Fabio cocked his head and then kept walking. "È bella, ma cattiva," he said, over his shoulder. She's beautiful, but mean.

LUCIA WAS PLANNING A GETAWAY, a surreptitious break from her mother's grip. Emanuele and I had convinced a man who owned a large home in Izzalini, the next town over, to rent her a studio apartment on the first floor.

The place was small—a water-stained bathroom, a cramped

kitchen, and a bedroom with windows that overlooked a patch of lawn and a quiet stretch of Via Todi—and furnished with a plastic table, a worn easy chair, and a mattress. I held Lucia's money so that her mother couldn't access it for the few days it would take her to save up something for the first month's rent, and we lent her the blue Twingo. While her mother was away one afternoon, Lucia loaded up the car with garbage bags full of clothing, a comforter, her father's old books, a bow and arrow, a bongo set, drumsticks, a pair of ragged old sneakers, and her slate gray cat. She arrived at our house jubilant.

"You're getting too involved," Serenella suggested, as I sat at her kitchen table, detailing our plans for Lucia.

"What else can we do?" I asked. "She's miserable at home."

Serenella said nothing more.

WE NAMED THE QUARTER HORSE Calamity Jane. After her first training session, Lucia slammed the stable door.

"È limitato," she said gravely. Limited.

"But *you* chose her," I said.

"Well, she's still a limited horse," Lucia said. "Paranoid, without respect."

"What does that mean?" I asked.

"It means you won't be able to ride her for a while, and even then, there are certain things she'll never be able to do."

Calamity Jane had resisted Lucia's approach, refusing to circle the rope, gaining strength each time Lucia slapped her with the stick.

Worse, we discovered that her ears were infected, covered in clumps of yellow fungus, which caused her tremendous pain when touched. When Lucia, Emanuele, or I reached for them to rub them with cream prescribed by Dr. Massarelli, she balked, heaving her massive weight about. As Lucia clung to one side, her hand edging closer to the ear, Calamity sidestepped violently out of her stall and across the barn, carrying Lucia with her, her ears pressed tight against her head, her nostrils letting out agitated snorts. Lucia flew toward the cement wall and slid to the ground. She looked up.

"You agreed to give me *carta bianca* with this horse," she said, fixing me with a hard glare.

Calamity trembled, steaming, in the corner, stomping her hooves.

I nodded. I still trusted Lucia.

NOW LUCIA WAS AT DINNER with us every night, at our house or at Casa Cruciani, sprawled on the couch, smoking her Lucky Strikes—her face more sunburned, her voice louder—and punching Ettore in the arm. She asked to borrow twenty euros, but when she got paid, she only bought herself more cigarettes. Every day I drove to find her at the restaurant. She was often angry, having fought with her boss for more money or more time, or having had to defend herself against the boss's accusations of her misbehavior as a daughter. Word spread fast; Lucia's mother painted herself the victim.

One midnight, Lucia called, weeping, from her studio. The slate gray cat had escaped, and Lucia had run after it, locking herself out. Emanuele and I drove over in the dark with an x-ray sheet from when Ettore had broken his thigh falling from Daisy. Lucia was in tears on her front stoop, and the cat was nowhere to be seen. Emanuele and I tried to jimmy open the door with the x-ray sheet; we slid it in and out, the hazy image of a bone growing crinkled. It had opened our locked door before, but it didn't work here. Finally, we knocked on the door of the nearby bakery, where a bewildered baker, kneading bread at one in the morning, looked up the landlord's phone number in his yellow pages. Lucia was deeply apologetic, but she'd do the same thing again at least three times. She gathered up a collection of sympathetic figures—mostly single, deprived men of various ages, and, well, me—and called on them for favors, for rides, for money, for meals, time and again.

She gained everyone's affection, with her sorry story and her agrarian talents. When Giamo the Macedonian helped milk the Crucianis' sheep, Lucia stepped into the pen and asked to learn the trade. On the first try, she clamped the ewe between her forcible thighs and bent beneath it, deftly squeezing out milk.

"How fun!" she explained, flashing her crooked grin and ushering another ewe beneath her as I stood outside the pen, my hands pressed against the wire.

THE TOWN GATHERED DAILY TO watch Lucia's sessions with Calamity, because it was better than sitting outside the bar. Out in the field, with the audience of men and women leaning against one another, Lucia, with the *carta bianca* I had bestowed upon her, sparred with Calamity. It was not like her time with Tallulah, the gentle, forceful dance between an animal and a person. At first, it was strained—Lucia was stern, commanding. And then, one day, it turned brutal, like some ultimate fight between horse and woman.

When I got to the field, after feeding Marcus and picking the mud from Daisy's hooves, Lucia was already wearing a muddy, torn white tank top and a cap and was holding a long black whip. She was whipping Calamity, who was connected to her by a rope and a bitless halter. When Calamity stepped away, Lucia forced her back. If Calamity threw herself into the air, Lucia slapped her harder with the whip. When the horse came at her, she punched it in the shoulder, sending it high-stepping back. They were both dripping with sweat, breathing heavily. The crowd was silent, chattering sometimes about school or work and then looking back at Lucia when someone else whispered, "Silenzio." The horse was steaming, plumes of condensation rising up from her coat. The whites of her eyes showed.

"Stronza!" Lucia shouted, red faced, as Calamity disobeyed her again. And the two continued their fight until the sun set.

The dogs in the cage on the hillside, the ones who were chained to their doghouses behind mesh, including the one who had nearly hung himself trying to chase Marcus, barked at the spectators, and Ettore, bored, ran up to them, kicking at them through the cage.

"They need to know respect," he said, laughing.

I raced up behind and grabbed his upper arm, pulling him back.

"Scemo, basta, basta!" I shouted, my eyes tearing. You idiot, enough, enough!

The crowd quieted and stared at me. My body tightened up. Ettore looked at me, surprised, a little embarrassed. He had been putting on a show for everyone.

"O, Giustina, calma," he said. "They need to know to fear man."

"Not like that, you damn moron," I said, my voice high. Ettore regarded me, befuddled, and I stared straight at him, my lower lip trembling.

"Hey, Giustina, come back down here," someone said, and I walked down to where everyone was gathered and called Marcus over to me. She sat firmly on my lap, her chest taut as always, poised like a little spring ready to launch, and I rested my head on top of hers and watched Lucia and Calamity spar.

When Calamity entered her stall that day, she hung her head, and her eyes were dull.

"This isn't a good idea," I said to Emanuele that night. "Lucia was too rough with Calamity today."

"This is how you shape a horse," Emanuele said. "Otherwise, Calamity will be too dangerous."

"There must be another way," I said. But I didn't know what it was.

A few days later, Calamity swiftly kicked her back haunch out as Lucia approached. I heard the deep clack of hoof against bone, and Lucia hit the ground. Calamity had struck her directly on the hip bone. The only physical proof was a pinprick of blood popping out onto the skin. Somewhere, in a crevice of the blackest part of my heart, I was happy.

Lucia wrapped her arm around my shoulders, wincing, letting out little cries, and I dragged us up to the car and drove us to the dingy emergency room in Todi, where an unfortunate group of people languished on plastic chairs. There was no receptionist, and the doors that led into the facility were locked. A Pakistani medic, clad in fluorescent orange, with a scar running straight down his nose, popped his head in every ten minutes.

Once Lucia had been called and had limped off into the depths of the hospital, I sat up very straight. Perhaps I never wished to ride a horse again, if this was how horses were shaped. I had known that these horse shenanigans were a bad idea, but I'd pressed on, and look where it had gotten me: miserably entangled in a bunch of bad situations, sitting in a dilapidated emergency room in Todi.

THAT NIGHT, I DREAMED OF a Doberman pinscher with floppy ears lying in the piazza, wearing a suit of armor that had fallen loosely to the side. Underneath, he was skin and bones, and I did not know what to do or whom to call. At dawn, Marcus woke me by shaking her body, flapping her ears against her head. I put on my sneakers and ran through the town with her beside me. I had hated running before that spring, and in my life had never conquered more than the single timed mile required for elementary school students. Now, I found that I had to run every morning in order to maintain some semblance of composure during the day.

I ran a low path through the woods in the dim morning light, regretting every choice I'd made and my own ignorance in the face of the horses, in the face of Umbria. I had missed the essence and complexity of the place and of the animals. I had never bothered to consider the world into which I was bringing Calamity. I had simply wanted a horse, another lovely pet, and now I had one, but it wasn't what I'd expected.

I had assumed that because Lucia claimed to know horses, and because the people of Collelungo supported her claim, it was true. I had allowed her to become the commander of a life, and I had never wondered if she was truly qualified. I had done no research, read no books. I had believed that a horse was simply a beautiful vehicle, a fun, simple creature to transport me through the hills. Now, I wanted to allow Calamity to run free, but I owned no land. I knew of no horse rescue facilities. Moreover, though we referred to Calamity as my horse, she technically belonged to Emanuele; he had put forth most of the cash.

⁊

"A HORSE NEEDS TO TRUST in humans," Lucia said. An x-ray had shown no damage to the bone. A massive blue and purple bruise had bloomed on her hip. I wondered why, exactly, any horse in its right mind would trust us. I had seen Ettore smack Daisy with a rake and had yelled out, while even Lucia, who objected to such random physical violence, reacted with diplomatic calm.

"It's not effective," she said to him.

"It's monstrous!" I screamed, but Ettore just rolled his eyes. Since when were American women more dramatic than Italian ones?

One day, I walked into the barn to find Emanuele and Lucia employing an archaic but often-used method to teach a horse not to kick: They tied Calamity's teeth to her back legs, so that a kick would cause her pain. When she struggled, she cut her face and her shin, sharp red wounds from rope or a stray nail.

"Non mi piace," I said, shaking my head slowly. I don't like it. The image would never leave me.

"Do you have a better idea?" Lucia asked. "This is very basic horse training."

"It's too much," I said.

"If she kicks you, you'll be sorry," Lucia said, looking at me like I was a slow child.

"This is too much," I insisted, trying to maintain my composure.

"This is *la Doma Dolce*," Lucia said. A gentle style of training.

"Non è la Doma Dolce," I said to Ettore.

"You would not survive a minute watching a normal horse tamer," Ettore said. "You don't want to know what they do."

No, I didn't. The two of them untied Calamity, who stood, broken, in her pen. She still kicked. Nobody wanted to go near her.

Lucia did not tie Calamity up again, but she continued to attempt to shape the horse. She spent an hour in the center of town one day, heavy in the saddle, forcing Calamity to step into a dark area where the shadow hit the asphalt. The horse was horrified and rebellious; the shadow, in her twisted brain, was dangerous, and she could not enter into it, but Lucia hoped to pull her out of the mindset. *I vecchi* stood by, murmuring to each other about this insane horse and the insane girl on it, and a frightened lady called the police to report a disturbance.

"I knew the horse was mad the day I met her," Fabio said. He still fed her oats in the mornings. "You can see it on her face."

I couldn't see it, though I looked. I could only see this animal that stood all day in a stall, waiting for people to come and begin the torture. There was no relief for anyone: Emanuele had spent his savings on this horse, and now its reputation preceded it. Nobody in the area would step near Calamity, so he could not pawn her off.

"Give her away," I pleaded. "Give her to somebody who will keep her at their house, just to look pretty outside."

"I can't," Emanuele said. "She was all my money."

"Is there somewhere else we can send her to learn?" I asked.

"The only place in the area is much tougher than Lucia," Emanuele said. "Even Ettore cannot watch what they do."

We began to search for someone to take her, either to breed her or to leave her alone in a pasture. Emanuele was willing to take a significant loss, since Calamity was unrideable, dejected, and eating up the hay.

I fed her carrots every day, holding out my palm so that she could pluck them gently from it and chew, and come back again to touch her soft muzzle to me. But I was frightened of her, of her unpredictable spurts of violence, so I rarely led her to pasture. She was no longer permitted to run free. Nobody wished to hold her rope and let her graze; she had tried to flee before. So she stayed inside.

"Mi dispiace," I said, but it was an empty apology. I could not save her; I could hardly look at her.

I was somebody who had always gotten things done. Once I narrowed in on a need or desire, I was unstoppable in my quest to satisfy it. I made appointments on time, found the lowest price, the best doctor, the perfect café. The solution to every problem lay in indefatigable research, in action, in focus. But here, faced with perhaps the most substantial quandary of my life—one that involved another living being—I was helpless. Collelungo was not New York, or Detroit or Iowa City or even Rome. No amount of time on the Internet could bring me to an answer for Calamity—the Italian backcountry didn't function that way. I did not have the linguistic fluidity or resources to start making inquisitive phone calls about rescue facilities or possible buyers.

Six months later, Emanuele would finally trade Calamity for a pair of calves, and she would live, unbothered, as a decoration in a paddock a few towns over. But that was not to my credit; in the end, I did nothing for her.

I did not wish to fail Marcus, too. It was one of the reasons

I remained in Collelungo: How could I possibly take Marcus to New York City? She wouldn't manage a day in that town.

❧

MEANWHILE, LUCIA, WHOM I HAD invited to Collelungo, had burrowed in. Now, the horses belonged more to her than to me, and she was able to take them out whenever she wished. While Emanuele worked at the English mansion, Lucia worked, too: painting doors, mowing the lawn, trimming the trees. She stripped herself of her shirt and worked in a swimsuit top, her body turning brown. She steadied a heavy drill by herself, her arms pressing down as it shook into the ground. She stripped down to her underwear and jumped into the pool, hollering and giggling, and then pulled herself out and went back to work, sweating in the midday heat, her forehead crunched up in concentration. In the afternoons, Emanuele dropped her at work. I had begun to refuse to act as her chauffeur, but she had befriended the locals in a way I never could and had managed to convince them to cart her about. So she was everywhere, and I was fading out.

One day, I had been calling Emanuele, but he did not pick up. I sat in the house with the Crucianis in their spots: Fabio watching television, Serenella at the stove, Alessandra wandering with Francesco, his fat hand gripping an adult hand above, always laughing. Marcus was in the woods, chasing chipmunks. I was on the couch, reading *How to Be Your Dog's Best Friend,* which my mother had sent me. I translated the title into Italian, and Serenella let out a heavy sigh.

"Hey, Giustina, my wife wants to leave me," said Fabio, to distract me. Whenever I was quietly sad, even when I hoped to hide it, I saw Fabio peeking at me with a wash of concern spread across his wrinkled face. He held *il sigaro infinito* in his hand.

"Yes, I do," Serenella said, standing in the kitchen.

"Is it because you don't do anything around here?" I asked.

"Sì!" Fabio said.

"What will you do if your wife leaves you?"

"Eh, beh," he said, smiling. "I'll go into the convent."

"You're too old for the convent," I said.

"Oh goodness, Giustina, you are never too old for the convent!"

Finally, I heard the rumble of a car and opened the door. There was the Englishman's sports car, Le Spider. It was a low, black European-brand car that the Englishman had already once crashed into a tree while driving drunk in the rain at top speed. Now, Emanuele had to warm up the car every few weeks to keep it in good condition. It pulled up into the driveway, and I peered out to see Emanuele and Lucia there, seated in the leather bucket seats, happily smoking their cigarettes.

"You didn't answer your phone," I said upon greeting.

"I didn't hear it," he said.

Lucia offered me her broad smile, and they both walked by. I sat seething on a chair, looking down at the blurred and meaningless words in *How to Be Your Dog's Best Friend.* There was Lucia, sitting on the fireplace, chattering on as Emanuele rocked Francesco. The night before, the only night I had ever gone out on my own—to join English-speaking Sabrina and her American friend in Perugia— Lucia had joined the Crucianis for pizza, and had sat in my chair.

"Vieni qua," I said suddenly to Emanuele, who looked at me blankly from the sofa. The room went very quiet, and everyone froze in place, staring at me. "Vieni qua!" I repeated, my voice suddenly shrill, trembling with anger. I stood at the door.

Outside, I looked at his impassive face. "What is she doing here? With you, in the car?"

"You are hard, like Hitler," Emanuele said in English.

"Excuse me?"

"You just called me like a dog," he said, still speaking English. "Everyone marvel at how you talk to people," he said.

I felt the color drain from my face. I had learned the wrong Italian, country Italian, and now I spoke without nuance or subtlety. I ordered my boyfriend around like one of history's most gruesome, genocidal, uniquely mustachioed dictators? Everyone marveled at my speech? At how terrible I sounded?

"Nobody says anything, but I see it in their eyes," he said.

"I don't know the system," I said softly.

"Well, it's sweetness and patience," he said, and walked back into the house.

THE NEXT DAY, UNRECOVERED BUT poker-faced, I went to a horse fair called I Nitriti di Primavera, or the Neighs of Spring. Emanuele and I slid into the cramped back of his friend Lollo's turquoise Mini Cooper, and we took off. I debated bringing Marcus along but decided that she might have a panic attack with all the commotion; I had recently witnessed her hyperventilate when she was asked, in a particularly full car, to sit on my lap instead of under the seat. Since nobody would take her for a walk, I couldn't leave her in the house. I put her in the pen—now overgrown with weeds—in which she had lived before.

The Neighs of Spring took place on some fairgrounds a half hour from Rome. It was a series of shows: jumping, dressage, reining, cutting. In one ring, a pair of draft horses slowly pulled a carriage in which sat a man and a woman, each dressed in baroque faux silk period costume. In another ring, children rode ponies. A group of people, all in the same outfit of jodhpurs, high boots, a lace-collared blouse, and a black fedora, took turns riding their nearly identical tall horses through an obstacle course.

Many attendees had brought their dogs, which trotted happily about on leashes, and I immediately felt a pang of regret and longing. Without Marcus, I had begun to feel mildly incomplete, a gnawing sense of dissatisfaction. Though I knew a young woman should be enjoying a more raucous social life, I couldn't help wanting to be home with my dog. More distressing at the moment, I was having an intense allergic reaction to the fairground. This was hay fever on steroids: My eyes had swelled up, my nose was dripping, and I sneezed every thirty seconds. I had purchased prescription-grade antihistamines at the *farmacia* in Morre and began to treat them like Tic Tacs, to no avail. I stuffed my purse with napkins, which I used to blot the tears from my eyes and sneeze into, and I ambled around the stands that sold all manner of American western wear, from intricate silver belt buckles to silk wild rags to bolo ties. There were stands full of cowboy hats and boots, plaid shirts and Wrangler jeans. The overdose of allergy pills, while ineffective at treating any actual allergies, allowed me a level of disconnect, and I stared in wonder at the mass of Italians dressed like tidy cowboys, obliviously trying on Confederate-flag belt buckles.

"I know you've heard of spaghetti westerns," Ettore said as he pulled on a pair of suede chaps lined with fringe.

After aimlessly wandering around, disoriented by antihistamines, I bought myself a lemon ice drink and went to join the mass of Collelungese in the shade. Everyone was taking a rest during the height of the midday sun, and the dust from the ground stuck to our skin. There, in rare form, I slurped my drink and sneezed some more. I saw Emanuele, from whom I had been separated in the crowd, walking up. He sat down near me and then lay back on the patchy grass. Next, there was Lucia, lying down, too, and placing her head on his thigh, gazing up at the trees. I watched it all as if in a peaceful bubble and suddenly understood why a frustrated housewife might become addicted to prescription pills and then one day run her husband over with her luxury automobile.

After our siesta, we attended a performance by a trim, shirtless man who alternately stood atop an unsaddled horse and hung off its side as it circled a ring at top speed. His silky hair whipped around as he dangled from the sprinting animal, and it was impossible to see how, exactly, he was commanding it. After he was finished, four stunning young girls in gypsy dress performed a coordinated number with their horses. When we left, I slumped in the back of the Mini Cooper, still sneezing, and watched the fairgrounds disappear.

"Acqua frizzante?" Lollo asked, passing back a cool bottle of fizzy water.

The carbonation mixed with the multiple allergy pills in my system caused severe, shooting pains in my stomach. I was accidentally stoned and swollen; the only cure was to lie on my couch with Marcus nearby and figure out how to arrange a life in which I never again had to attend anything like the Neighs of Spring.

Upon my arrival, Marcus rejoiced, and so did I for one moment before I leaned in closer. I pulled her into the stable and sat down on the floor. My little spotted dog was covered in no fewer than two thousand black ticks. I held up her tail: a hundred ticks. I spread apart her toes: colonies of ticks. There were ticks in her ears, spread across her face, burrowing in across her pink belly, attached to her nipples, her eyebrows, the hair surrounding her paws. The weeds in the pen had been harboring perhaps millions of bloodsuckers during the high season. Certain sheep liked to wander in and take a nap, and this was also where Giamo milked the herd. The sheep were the ticks' most gracious hosts, and now Marcus, having spent a day there, may as well have been wearing a small cloak knit entirely of them.

I was compulsively picking them off one by one, dropping them into a jar full of alcohol, when Ettore came into the stable.

"Sei matta?" he asked. "You could get very sick from those ticks. That's not how you do it."

Emanuele joined him and they stood above me disapprovingly. I could die a brutal death of a tickborne disease if I didn't stop, according to them. If I didn't believe them, I could walk up the hill

and take a look at Lorenzo's mangled arm, which was currently gro-
tesquely infected.

"You have to use a powder," Ettore said. "I've done it twenty
times before."

Emanuele went to get me a repellent, and we covered Marcus
with the heavy yellow powder. I had begun to sniffle.

"What if we poison her?" I asked.

"Don't worry," Ettore said. "It will just make all the ticks fall
out. By tomorrow."

Up at the house, Serenella was concerned for Francesco. My
stomach still hurt.

"A tick bite could kill the baby!" she announced. "The dog
cannot be near the house."

"No, it's true," Emanuele said as I stomped outside; now, after
a solitary day, Marcus would have to spend the night by herself in
order to keep some random human baby entirely safe? What kind of
twisted priorities were these?

We put the horses out to pasture and contained Marcus in
Tallulah's stall. Marcus kept jumping out, scaling the four-foot door
with one nearly vertical jump, and trotting up to me, ready to return
home. Finally, Emanuele found some wood scraps and boarded up
the opening.

I was walking to the car when I started to weep, and passed on,
continuing into the wooded area that led down to the olive orchard.
I had never cried publicly in my entire life; I actually didn't think
I could. The place for crying was clearly behind locked bathroom
doors or in your mother's kitchen. But there in the middle of the
path, on that hot Umbrian day, I fell onto my knees and sobbed,
loudly, without restraint or embarrassment. I knelt in the woods and
wept, thinking about boarded-up little Marcus and how it was all
my fault, the poor horses and the poor dogs, and how I hated this
wretched place. Emanuele, Ettore, Zio Gianni, Lucia, and Marta

stood above me, uphill, regarding me like one might a wild and potentially dangerous animal in distress.

Finally, Emanuele approached slowly, bent down, and put forth an offer: "You get in the car, and I drive you home; then I will give Marcus water and her dinner."

Marta brought me a cup of chamomile tea, which she promised would soothe my stomach. Stripped of my will, I allowed myself to be led off like an invalid. I could see Serenella peering out at me from behind the kitchen window. She didn't look a bit surprised.

At home, I lay in bed, letting out moans and wiping my face while fielding several tentative text messages. *Come stai? Stai bene? Stai meglio?* How are you? Are you good? Are you better? They were concerned that the American had finally broken, and perhaps irreparably. The pharmacist had slipped Emanuele some relaxants once, so I popped two, downed another mug of chamomile, and floated off into sleep.

The next morning, I was no longer sneezing. I drove down to Marcus, who was dancing joyously in the boarded-up stall, definitely alive, pleased to see me, and surrounded by the scattered corpses of thousands of ticks. We embraced, though she was dusty with the residue of the tick killer, and I let her race through the pasture in her happy loops, and then, much to her chagrin, I took her home and bathed her, and left her in the house to get some rest.

I returned to the farm and found old, trustworthy Daisy. She was *buono come pane,* or good as bread, as Fabio said. I lured her to me from the open hill with a bucket of oats and saddled her. We followed the valley through Collelungo, through the village of Morre, and into the empty hills near Morruzze, which was the highest town for miles. It was a hot June morning, but the breeze offered moments of reprieve. For a distance, a good tamped-down-dirt galloping path opened—it stretched from the asphalt road to a vast villa with a grassy, gated pasture where a well-off Roman in retirement kept three hardy stock horses. As soon as we stepped onto the path, I pushed Daisy into a run, and I sat atop her, rocking back and forth with her body as we ascended, until we were gliding at top speed, Daisy pushing harder with each stride. Soon, we were surrounded by wildflowers growing high—white, pink, violet, untouched, stretching out for a mile. I could see to my right the entire valley below. We stopped at the peak, and I laid my head on Daisy's drenched neck, leaning into her mane, smelling her sweet, verdant, dirty scent. I looked out upon Morre and over into Collelungo, the sweeping patchwork hills and perfect stone houses, and the orchards and olive groves and just-tilled land, the breathtaking vista taken in from atop a white horse that was as good as bread. And I knew that more than anything in the world, I wanted to get the hell out of Italy.

WE KNOW THE TRUTH, NOT ONLY BY
THE REASON, BUT ALSO BY THE HEART.

—BLAISE PASCAL

ONE EARLY SUMMER MORNING BEFORE dawn, Emanuele's phone rang. An automated voice announced that the alarm at the Englishman's house had sounded. Without thinking, we dressed and sped along the dark roads.

The lock on the front gate had been snapped, and the doors of the house had been sawed through and thrown open. The house was alight and the windows shone, bright yellow rectangles in the blackness. Bianca, one of the guard dogs, was prancing around the property, delighted by the company. Meanwhile, Diego, the other guard dog, was hiding in his doghouse. The alarm rang loudly and continuously, but the house was far from its neighbors and the road. Two men remained inside, as far as we could tell, and Emanuele circled the property, honking, and then drove off to the main street, where a white van hurtled toward us, swerving so that we would not have time to see the license plate.

The men who had remained inside the house took off into the

forest, running on an alternate escape route, we guessed, and meeting the white van at some point where the main road wrapped
around on the other side. They had taken, a preliminary survey of
the house revealed, five fake Louis Vuitton suitcases, a small television, a few beers, three bottles of mediocre wine, and all of the
Englishman's pants, which, due to his jolly proportions, had been
tailored so that the waists were unusually wide and the legs unusually short. The telescope sitting by the door and the Gucci loafers
on the back lawn, which looked as though someone had stepped out
of them midstride, had been abandoned in the ruckus. I felt a little
bit sorry for the crooks, who had put so much effort into the robbery and had emerged with only some liquor and a pile of fat-man
trousers.

An hour after Emanuele made an emergency call, a sleepy pair
of policemen arrived from Todi. They ambled over to us as Bianca
barked viciously.

"Che bel cane," one of them said, and Bianca, identifying yet
another fine new friend, leaned against him for a caress.

It was now five a.m., and the rising sun cast a dim violet light
over the land. When the police were finished admiring the animal,
they wandered into the kitchen.

"Prendete un caffè?" Emanuele asked.

"Sì," one of the policemen said.

Meanwhile, the other dispassionately filled out a report that
would never be looked at, and perhaps would never even be filed. It
was an accepted fact that whatever the laws, in practice, the Italian
cops investigated nothing short of murder.

After this incident, the Englishman insisted that Emanuele
move into his house.

We moved out of the centro storico and into the isolated English mansion one town over.

"You know, I have to go back to America soon," I said as we packed up our boxes and replaced the multiple renderings of Gesù and Madre Maria. "Only for a few months."

"Yes, just until the winter," Emanuele said.

We both knew, however, that once I left, I'd never be back.

⁓

IT WAS EARLY JULY, WHEN the air grew dry and the grassy fields began to crackle and turn yellow. We were living in the Englishman's house, which was cavernous and unwelcoming. It had been a barn once, and the animal waste had permeated the stone floor in the basement, meaning that the place was always damp and cold. Emanuele and I took up residence in the guest room, which had high ceilings and no windows, just French doors that opened onto a small terrace. Marcus slept in a cramped basket in the corner and learned to bark from the guard dogs. She was nervous in the new place, and for a week after she acquired her new skills, she woke up at night with anxious yelps whenever she heard the slightest rustle. She spent her days running in the fields that stretched down off the swimming pool at the edge of the estate. She ran for hours, even under the scorching noonday sun, and returned at dusk. At night, I sat with Marcus on the lower level of the house, hoping that the Albanian thieves didn't show up in short, belted pants and kidnap me. Meanwhile, Emanuele played a seemingly endless game of cards at the bar. Marcus and I sat together on a soft chair, watching *Animal Cops* on the Englishman's satellite television. She slept, and I watched her snoring lightly, chasing sparrows even in her sleep, her paws twitching, her wet black nose turning from side to side, taking in a dream scent. I was making an impossible decision. I wanted out of this life; only one thing was keeping me from returning to my Brooklyn studio, and it was not Emanuele.

I HAD TO GIVE MARCUS away. It was the rational choice after so many irrational ones. Marcus would not survive a day in New York City. She was terrified of most people, loud noises, crowds, sidewalks, crinkled paper, men in hats, other dogs, flags and pinwheels, strange-looking chairs, statues large and small, unfamiliar rooms, her own reflection in a window. Really, she was terrified of nearly everything modern life had to offer. She derived her most fundamental joys from dashing through meadows and sniffing the heavy odor of quail and warblers nestled in bushes. An urban excursion would reduce her to a quivering mass of spotted fur; she could hardly stand to walk through Collelungo. But I had nowhere else to go: My mother lived in a four-hundred-square-foot studio uptown, from which even relaxed city dogs were prohibited. When I added Marcus to the equation, it drastically increased the difficulties I would face in returning to and living in America. Without her, I would be liberated, free to leave this freezing estate.

"You cannot keep yourself in a bad situation for the sake of a dog," my mother reasoned over the telephone.

"Above all, dogs are adaptable," my friend Sabrina said. "If someone else feeds her, she will be happy."

"I'll keep her," Emanuele said. But Marcus could hardly get up enough courage to approach him.

I decided that the only conceivable home for Marcus was with a family that was widely referred to as *i comunisti*, and that was where she would go.

I had first met one half of the Communist couple at Le Stelle. The male Communist, who was more accurately a hard-line socialist, was named Stefano. Stefano was a slender man of medium height whose metal eyeglasses rested upon his Roman nose. He wore a small, neatly trimmed white mustache, and his entire head was shaved daily, which gave him a very clean look. Stefano was fluent in German, and his English was adequate. When Emanuele introduced me, Stefano frowned.

"Did you vote for Bush?" he asked crisply as we shook hands. "Tell me something, what happened in the United States after 1987? Hey, you know one American I think is great? Phil Collins. Have you heard of the band Genesis?"

"Actually, I think Phil Collins is British," I said.

"Well, there goes that," said Stefano.

That evening, Emanuele and I attended a dinner at Stefano's house. His wife, Carlotta, whose round, pretty face was framed by long gray hair, balanced their pudgy son, Giacopo, on her hip. She and Stefano had migrated from Milan, and on this weekend, their Milanese friends had come for some time in the countryside. Carlotta and the rest of the women forwent bras and makeup. They were pale, with cracked lips and round hips. The women wore colorful corduroy pants or long Indian skirts. The men wore brown suede shoes, well-sculpted facial hair, and, if possible, ponytails.

"My American lover was from New York," one told me, her green eyes magnified behind thick glasses. "American men are so scared to live with a woman."

Carlotta was allergic to wheat, so she prepared a quinoa sea-food salad, which was unfortunate because Italians who did not grow up directly on the seashore lacked the ability to prepare fish. Worse, Umbrian supermarkets only sold their fish frozen, which turned it rubbery and pungent. But the Communists and their lib-eral friends were not particular, and they wore their intellectual shoes and ate their ancient-grain-and-octopus salad while discussing Marx, language, and political revolution.

I liked Carlotta and Stefano and their immense baby because they rejected provincial dicta and lived an unconventional life, which was rare in the area. The simple act of not dyeing your hair at thirty was a zealous show of rebellion, as evidenced by the ninety-five-year-old Collelungese sporting deep amber and jet black dos. Furthermore, Carlotta and Stefano owned three raggedy dogs, from whom they required no more than canine company. They kept dogs that performed no practical duties just because they really liked dogs. The noble shepherd mix Magoo had followed Stefano home through the streets of Milan. He belonged to another family, to which he would reluctantly return at night, after each day spent with Stefano. When the family decided to move away, Stefano kept Magoo. Pompeio, who matched a wild boar in size and texture, was a three-pound puppy when he peered up at Carlotta from a box on the street somewhere in Lazio. Mimoo, a fine young female husky, had been dropped at their doorstep by friends who moved from the icy northern mountains to an apartment in the city and no longer wanted her.

Carlotta and Stefano were dog people in a land lacking in dog people. I presented my case to Stefano: My beautiful pointer would perish without their help, and I could not stay in Italy forever. Would they consider adopting her?

He peered at me sympathetically through his wire-rimmed glasses.

"I'm an archaeologist," he said. "We have no money."

I would pay, I told him, for her food and care. He shook his head. "We have three already," he said. "Two are getting old and depressed."

"Marcus is young and pretty," I countered. "Perhaps she would please them?"

Stefano let out a pained sigh.

"She'll die with these farmers," I whispered. "You know that she'll die."

With that, the Communists agreed to take in Marcus.

I should have been relieved. Instead, every evening, I lay awake in the bedroom, looking up into the blackness, gripped by the gnawing sensation that I was doing something very wrong. But these were the emotional bonds from which I aimed to break free, so I willfully disregarded these suspicions and went forward with my plan, which, separated from mystical ideas about love and destiny, was a solid one.

Meanwhile, Marcus slept in her basket and leapt around in the wildflower field. She believed that she and I were a pack; she did not know that the leader of this pack of two was plotting her abandonment. I felt my chest tighten, but I tried to remember the reality of the situation: The life that awaited me in New York was not a life that would welcome a rural pointer, and where else could I sensibly go? This was the best solution for us both. In time, she would forget that I had ever existed, and she would live out her days in the peace of the countryside.

$$\sim$$

EVERY MORNING, FOLLOWING MY PROGRAM to habituate Marcus to her future home, we hiked through the woods to the Communists' compound. Their house sat in a parcel on the outskirts of Camerata. To get there from the English house, we crossed an open field and then entered the wilderness, plodding over a muddy path and emerging at a deserted hut. The Communists lived in a run-down two-story farmhouse set far off the main road. To arrive by car, you had to drive over a bumpy dirt lane, past a vacant chicken coop, and up into the thick woods. There, a small patch of lawn surrounded by a high fence had been slashed from the forest.

The house was unremarkable except that it was dirty for an Italian home. There was no immaculate rose garden in the front, no neat stone walkway. Instead of the just-scrubbed terra-cotta floors and freshly waxed tables of Collelungo's families, the Communist house was covered in a thin layer of dust. The place was scattered with hats, towels, bowls, dinosaur toys, boxes of tea, mugs, potato chips, chewing bones, shoes, rain slickers, nubby knit blankets, ragged manuscripts, and beach balls. There was no blaring TV. There were impossible-to-find staircases that led up to dusty nooks stuffed with beds.

The main room was a cold space with few windows. Low-slung

couches covered in Guatemalan blankets were pressed against the walls, and a long oak table ran the length of one side. A wan fire burned in a massive fireplace filled with piles of ash. Here, in the home of Communists, everyone was equal, which meant that the dogs were permitted on the couches and chairs. Their mixed fur coated most surfaces.

"It's just impossible to keep clean," Carlotta said from behind a pile of papers on the kitchen table. Despite her protests, she was a halfhearted housekeeper—the sort who waved a feather duster at a bookshelf for three minutes before becoming distracted—and preferred to rock her baby in her arms, to drive him around in her red jalopy, showing him the neighbors' sheep and pigs, and to read novels and poetry.

I hoped that my daily visits would acclimate Marcus to her new home. I hoped that she would play with the dogs, and they would form a warm friendship that would nurture them all and bind them together. Instead, the female husky despised Marcus and chased her about, snarling, and the two male mutts ignored her, choosing instead to lie in silence in a sun spot on the patchy front lawn, perhaps reflecting on better days, a doggy approximation of *i vecchi*. Carlotta continued to carry her child around the house, feeding him handfuls of pretzels and speaking to him in hushed tones. The child had a mess of blond hair, a squeezable face, and two front teeth poking through his gums. He let out delighted gurgles when the dogs rushed by. His legs looked like enormous bratwursts poking out from his diaper, and he toddled through the kitchen barefoot, always ravenous.

Though Stefano had unenthusiastically agreed to Marcus's adoption, he did not like the idea of four disconnected strays thrown together in his backyard. He had hoped that little Marcus, with her femininity and verve, would boost the spirits of his aging mutts. But they didn't care for Marcus one way or another.

"Perhaps if she had not been spayed," Stefano offered dolefully. "Perhaps then she would have helped Magoo feel a bit younger, more vigorous." Marcus eyed Stefano fearfully from afar.

Still, compelled by shaky optimism and urgency, I made my daily pilgrimage, holding out hope that eventually Marcus would get used to the place. She had to, because I had booked a ticket to New York City, leaving in six weeks.

One day in the middle of July, at five in the evening, I decided to leave Marcus alone at the Communists' house. It was possible that she was merely distracted by my presence, and if I was gone, she might attend to Carlotta or befriend one of the mutts. Moreover, we needed to begin our separation. Slowly slowly, as the Italians said. *Piano, piano.*

Marcus was on her usual romp through the back field as I edged toward the front gate. Then, just as I opened it, she was beside me, trying to push her way through with me.

"You stay here," I commanded, and she backed up and cocked her head.

I closed the gate behind me and turned around. Marcus stood still, watching me in disbelief, her black nose balanced on a gap in the fence, her brown eyes rounder than ever before. I trudged up the hill and out into an open area where a new house had just been built. Some of the Communists' friends from Milan had decided to make their own urban exodus, and they had constructed a place nearby. Outside, a child's party was taking place. There was a Slip 'n Slide on the lawn, and an inflatable dipping pool filled with water. Two plastic tables sat by the door, laid out with baskets of cookies. There were also two large watermelons, carved into slabs, the pink pieces dripping juice off the tables. A dozen children circled the grass. The adults sat, drinking wine, water, and soda, with one of them occasionally jumping up to pluck a baby from a pool or to pull two children apart. They motioned me over, and I joined them for a piece of fruit. The sky was striped with yellow and violet, and evening was near. I headed back down the hill.

Forty-five minutes later, I found Marcus exactly where I had left her, nose balanced in the gap in the fence, eyes fixed in my direction. When she saw me, she began to celebrate, shaking with relief, and when I opened the gate, she clutched me with her front paws, pressing her face to me and breathing in my scent. Carlotta emerged from the house and crossed the lawn.

"She stood there the entire time, even when I went out to comfort her," Carlotta said. "She was inconsolable. It was almost an hour."

I slumped down on the ground, and Marcus leaned in to me and let out the sigh of homecoming, her nose raised, twitching.

"Carlotta, what do I do?" I asked.

"I'll keep the dog for you," Carlotta said, looking down at us. She wore a long skirt, and the setting sun caught the silver in her hair. "But it won't be my dog."

I rested my chin on the back of Marcus's neck and took in that familiar musky smell.

"If you ask me, an owner does not choose its dog; a dog chooses its owner," Carlotta said. "And this dog has chosen you."

Carlotta was turning back to get the baby, who was naked, playing with pebbles.

I had hoped to find a great love in Italy, to find a new place and a new way to live. Then, assuming that I had finally, irrevocably failed in my quest, I'd decided to take off. I had moped about, convinced that in many ways this whole journey had been one giant failure. But how *stupida* was I? Here was my new way to live, my unknown new place, and my great Italian love. Meanwhile, I was trying my hardest to give her away so that I could return to a life that I knew but didn't much care for.

I stood up and told Carlotta that she didn't have to worry, Marcus would be coming back to America with me.

SOMETIMES I GO ABOUT IN PITY
FOR MYSELF, AND ALL THE WHILE,
A GREAT WIND CARRIES ME
ACROSS THE SKY.

—OJIBWA SAYING

EMANUELE AND I LEFT THE English house when the Englishman and his family arrived for vacation. There, we parted. He
returned home to Fabio and Serenella, to the nest. I wrote a friend
who lived on an island off the coast of Massachusetts. She could
make space for us briefly in August. I had not been able to devise
any further plans.

I scoured the countryside for a place to stay. Nobody would take
a woman and her dog. Finally, I came upon an *agriturismo*—a dis-
tinctly Italian farm-guesthouse combination—called Il Capricorno,
in the outskirts of nearby Acqualoreto. It was owned by a woman
named Tiziana, who lived there alone with her German shepherd,
Lia. For a month, Marcus and I took a small, spotless room on the
second floor. The green metal shutters opened to silent orchards.
Marcus ran in the woods during the day, returning dusty and tired in
time for dinner.

For a week, a couple of Roman octogenarians on their annual country holiday stayed in a room next to mine. They were dignified and urbane, each with white hair, tan skin, and large, shiny teeth. They had been married for fifty-four years. The wife was particularly fascinated that I had dated a farmer, and continued to question me on my choice, observing the obvious impossibility of the situation.

"It is different worlds," she announced, aghast. "Different levels!"

For the most part, it was me and Tiziana, Marcus and Lia. Tiziana baked loaves of brown bread for breakfast. Every morning she left for work, cleaning houses in Orvieto. In the evening, we ate dinner together and sometimes sat on the patio at dusk with glasses of white wine, while Marcus and Lia raced around the fruit trees. Tiziana was curvy and soft, with milky skin and short brown curls. She read horror novels and books about guardian angels. She was dating a policeman she had met online. She had a family of goats, a coop of chickens, olive trees, and lemon groves.

One night, Tiziana told me that she had fallen gravely ill when she was younger. At her lowest point, the image of a saint had come to her. She claimed that she saw him as clearly as she saw me standing before her, this dead saint, whose photograph was posted on the wall: your average modern-day saint, in a dark cloak, with a silver beard. He stood beside her, and the next day, her chronic condition fell away. The medication began to work. Her misery dissipated. She was able again to take care of the garden.

"Since that day, people who come here notice that it's a very peaceful place," she said. "I was lying in your bedroom when I saw the saint. I bet you get a good night's sleep there."

I did sleep better there than anywhere I'd ever stayed.

Tiziana was still managing her condition; if she didn't take medicine daily, she would have a stroke.

"Aren't you scared?" I asked.

She was not scared of death or illness. She had known a one-hundred-year-old man, she told me, and she had asked him what it was like to reach such an old age. He told her to go to the window, so she went to the window. He told her to open it, which she did, and then he told her to close it, which she also did.

"That's my life," the man said.

⤜⤏

FINALLY, MARCUS AND I LEFT. I had not seen the Cruciani family much since I had moved to Acqualoreto, but when I did stop in to say good-bye, they were casual, and we all pretended, unconvincingly, that I would be back in a few months to visit. We said "*arrivederci*," which means, literally, "until we meet again." Nobody said "*addio*," which really means good-bye, forever.

"Ti voglio bene," Alessandra said, putting her arms around me. The Italian term for unromantic love: I want you well.

"Do you need some food for the road?" Serenella asked, dragging on her long cigarette.

Fabio kissed me on the cheek and then followed me to the door.

"Ciao, Giustina," he said. He stood very still in the doorway of the white stucco house with a look of sorrow on his dark face, wearing an untucked blue button-down, *il sigaro infinito* resting on his lip. From the distance, as we drove out of the drive and began to descend Via Todi, I could see his silhouette carved out by the light behind him.

Emanuele, whom I had seen only briefly near the end, drove me to the airport and gave me a letter, written with black ballpoint on a white sheet of computer paper. It began, in Italian: *Non sono stato l'uomo della tua vita, ma sono stato il tuo compagno di viaggio per un lungo, difficile, ma bellissimo anno.* I am not the man of your life, but I have been your companion on a long, difficult, but very beautiful year.

At Fiumicino, I stood on the tarmac while everyone boarded the plane. In the distance, a motorized cart was hurtling toward us. LIVE ANIMALS, the cart said. Inside, curled up in a beige crate, lay Marcus. She looked at me, shocked by her current predicament.

"I'm an animal lover, too," a young worker said, sidling up to me as his colleagues loaded her into the cargo hold.

"Will she be okay?" I asked.

"Let's just say she'd be better at home," the worker said. "But she'll survive."

I boarded the plane, and landed in Boston, where I collected a catatonic Marcus, still perched in her beige crate, from the baggage claim. Over the next day, we made our way to the island, Marcus leaning her trembling spotted body on me wherever we went—on the ferry, down the street—until we reached our destination.

People cried out from the sidewalk, "That's one flipped-out dog!"

I wanted to tell those jerks a thing or two about Marcus's history and her talents. I bet their smiling New England animals of privilege, chilling out on the streets, couldn't stalk and kill six (that's right, *six*) chickens. I bet their dogs couldn't chase a horse for twenty miles. And their dogs probably hadn't spent the first years of their lives in a pen, with dry kibble to eat and green sludge to drink. They had also not just hurtled through the air from one continent to another, stuffed in a plastic box.

Instead of picking a fight with an innocent stranger, I took Marcus to the wide ocean beach, which she had never before seen. At first, she attempted to return to the car, touching her paws gingerly to the sand and then pulling back.

"I promise you'll like it," I said, and nudged her along.

Once there, she spotted swarms of birds standing about, as though awaiting her arrival, and her heart rose. Perhaps she was beginning to believe that I really knew what I was talking about.

Perhaps she was thinking that her trip through the sky was worth it after all. I bent down and unclasped her leash. She stood near me for a moment, her black nose high, taking in air. Then she looked up at me expectantly, and I motioned her forward.

Marcus crouched into her hunting pose and began her slow stalk toward the gulls, the plovers, the sandpipers. When she was nearly close enough to nibble a tasty little wing, the birds took off en masse, and she ran behind them with her mouth open in that canine smile, her teeth showing, sprinting at top speed. She matched their aerial swoops on land and dipped her paws in the Atlantic. People on the beach, witnessing this side of Marcus, approached me. They wanted to know where they could acquire such a remarkable dog.

I could not even begin to explain.

ACKNOWLEDGMENTS

ﾑ

I AM FIRST INDEBTED TO my high school English teacher James Bucar who, more than anyone before or since, taught me how to write. I was also encouraged by my New York University professor Stacy Pies and by my professional mentor Catherine Kelley. The writer Ted Kerasote provided me with invaluable insight into the world of publishing. Throughout this whole process, my too-often faraway friends Jennifer Fields, Kate Garrick, Anna Godbersen, Gina Hamadey, Vanessa Horvath, Scott Korb, Julia Langbein, Marta Nini, and Anna Stein have provided company, inspiration, humor, freelance work, and fried chicken. The talented and patient André Mora helped me through the writing process and then drew me a gorgeous cover. I am also lucky to have an editor as smart and intuitive as Shannon Welch.

I am forever grateful to those remarkable people who helped me when I needed it most, and asked for nothing in return. Tiziana Barbieri allowed me and Marcus into her beautiful Il Capricorno Agriturismo. Diane Reverand and Sol Slotnik graciously welcomed us into their rambling colonial estate and didn't get too mad when

ACKNOWLEDGMENTS

Marcus muddied the cream carpet with her pawprints. The generous Michael Denslow, Emily Herrick, and Lucie took me in time and again, cooked me slow-food dinners, and proved that sometimes, without reason, strangers become family. Samuel Choritz looked after Marcus and me and made our duo into a trio. Nikki Wood, the compassionate and brilliant dog behaviorist at Hamptons Dog Training, worked tirelessly and without compensation to help turn a scared farm dog into a cheery, if nervous, little member of society. Without Nikki, there would be no happy ending to this unusual Italian love story; she enabled me to maintain one of the richest, most vivid relationships I have ever had.

There are two families I must thank. The first is the Cruciani family: Fabio, Serenella, Alessandra, Ettore, Paolo, Franci, and Emanuele: *Avete condiviso le vostre vite con me e mi avete insegnato più di quel che potreste mai immaginare. Vi ringrazio dal profondo del mio cuore.* The second family is my own: my cheerleader, my confidante, my advisor, my lifelong best friend—and, these days, my literary agent: my mother, Patricia van der Leun.